WINNING THE WAR WITHIN

PTSD AND THE LONG ROAD HOME

Presented by

KATIE BELL

ii

WINNING THE WAR WITHIN

PTSD AND THE LONG ROAD HOME

BY

BRENTON MACKINNON

Published by
Bookstand Publishing
Morgan Hill, CA 95037
3083_2

ISBN 978-1-58909-689-9

Printed in the United States of America

iv

"War fosters an impossible collection of opposites: murder, soldiery comradeship, torture, religious conviction, the destruction of the earth, patriotism, annihilation, and hope for immortal glory. Wartime seems to propel life to its most vivid, most meaningful level. Engaged in the activity of destruction, its soldiers and its victims discover a profound sense of existing, of being human."

A Terrible Love of War
James Hillman

"And every night when I dream,
I hear the men and the monkeys
In the jungle scream."

Drive On
Johnny Cash

PREFACE

What follows is not offered as an excuse to the people I have offended, wives I left, children I didn't parent, or the credit card company I still owe. This is just a story, not unlike many others, and for the most part, true. Names have not been changed to protect the incompetent, including my own.

Should the present generation of veterans and families find something of value herein, then those of us who have preceded you may find some measure of consolation.

The history of our humankind is a history of war. Conflict continues as I write this and will, as you read this.

Teach your children well...

ACKNOWLEDGEMENTS

These many decades have been filled with family, friends and fellow travelers, most with loving hearts and open minds. Without them, I would have joined the many veterans who survived Vietnam, but not the coming home.

My eternal thanks to my daughter, Nova, who has created and shared what I could not: family. And thanks to you, Edmund, my estranged son, conceived at a PTSD conference and a victim in the aftermath.

None of this would have been possible without the encouragement of the following rascals (please don't hold them responsible): Bob, Frank, Sandy, Julia, Tom, Andrea, Kenny, Janet, Wally, Rick, Tony, Andy, Martin, Captain John, Hud, Herb, and Debbie.

Of course, as any soldier in any foxhole, anywhere, will gratefully acknowledge, thank you, Mom.

x

Table of Contents

PREFACE   vii

ACKNOWLEDGEMENTS   ix

PART ONE   1
THE HERO's JOURNEY IN FOUR EASY
STEPS   3
    I Fantasy Island, Malibu, CA, 1965   3
    II Human Sacrifice, Berkeley, CA, 1965   7
    III Patriot, San Diego, CA, 1966   11
    IV Return of the Naïve, Berkeley, CA,
    1966   13
The Three Wise Men, Defense Language Institute,
Monterey, CA, Fall, 1966   15

PART TWO   23
Vietnamese Playboy, An Hoa, Vietnam, 1967   25
Gladiator, Battle of Union II, Vietnam, June 2,
1967   29
The Walking Dead, An Hoa Base, Vietnam,
June 5, 1967   33
Man's Best Friend, Phu Loc 6 Outpose,
Vietnam, 1967   36
Major Principal, An Hoa, Vietnam, 1967   43
The Great Race, Quang Tri, Vietnam, 1967   49
NONG SON TRILOGY   53
    I False Memory?, Reno, NV, 1995   53

Table of Contents (continued)

II Teacher, Translator, Soldier, Spy, An Hoa, Vietnam, 1967   58

III Monsoon, Nong Son, Vietnam, 1967   62

PART THREE   67

Full Circle, Bellaire, TX, 1969   69

INTELLIGENCE TRILOGY   76

I No Escape, Bamako, Mali, Africa, 1974   76

II The Long Yesterday, Nong Son, Village, Vietnam, 1967   78

III Back in Bamako, Mali, Africa, 1974   81

How Shakespeare Saved My Life, Sonoma State University, CA, 1974   82

Gook Lover, Graduate School, Fredonia, New York, 1981   89

The Diary of Vinh Lu, Quang Tri Provence, Vietnam   91

Common Ground, Soviet Union, 1988   106

PART FOUR   123

Reunion!, Long Beach, CA, 1989   126

Veterans All, Marin County, CA, 1993   130

Second Homecoming, Nong Son, Vietnam, 1999   139

PTSD QUARTET   147

I Emotional Hygiene, Marin County, CA, Ongoing…   147

Table of Contents (concluded)

II "It Ain't My Fault!", Marin County, CA,
Ongoing…   151

III Seasoning, Marin County, CA,
Ongoing…   155

IV Listening Skills, Marin County, CA,
Ongoing…   160

Lament for Brother D   162

Shadows, Sarge Remembers   165

POEMS   **171**

Chips in the Mint
    "More Ice Cream, Honey?"   171

John Kerry Has a Cup of Coffee
    "Refill, Darlin?"   173

John McCain Pretends, *Maverick*
    "Dad's fault…"   177

Sons of Abraham
    "This Gaza trip"   179

Welcome Home
    "Only the feathers floating…"   180

The Long Road Home
    "Broken home"   182

EPILOGUE   **185**

ABOUT THE BOOK   **186**

ABOUT THE AUTHOR   **186**

PART ONE

Wouldn't it be great if American high schools taught the principles of ethics, morals, and yes, even critical thinking? In the midst of chaos and confusion, we would know not only what is right or wrong, good or bad, but why. In time of war, we would have already decided what is worth fighting for, worth killing for, and what might be - worth dying for.

In 1961, my peer group focused on sports, and struggled with the transition between adolescence and that illusive American destination: manhood. All around us, suburban fathers commuted to work each morning and returned to an evening of pot roast, martinis, and television.

With no alternative life styles, roles, or personalities modeled for us, the only access to a different universe trickled through movies and the pages of adventure novels. Why not run around the planet and accumulate exotic and interesting experiences? If enough chapters played out, or if you stumbled into some sort of revelation, not only an interesting life style but the meaning of life itself, might be magically revealed.

As my friends migrated to career tracks as doctors, lawyers, and dentists, the known world held no appeal for me. I stood at the crossroads. Men over the age of eighteen in my generation faced a military draft. By twenty-three I had attended two colleges, worked as a furniture deliveryman, bicycle mechanic, dish washer, busboy, life guard, dive shop salesman, night watchman for a veterinarian, steel mill worker, mail sorter, drug store deliveryman, art presentation coordinator and ambulance attendant; the perfect resume for cannon fodder.

These many experiences created a perception that the single most important qualification for success in a job was - willingness. Most jobs could be learned in only a few days or weeks. Interchangeable scenarios inflated my confidence and fueled an existential notion that the same basic human melodrama and personality types waited just around the corner. Jobs, colleges, relationships, and geography all blurred together as entertaining distractions and a temporary remedy for a deeper longing I had yet to recognize.

What to do? Choosing not to act can be as powerful and consequential an impulsive decision. If we wait, maybe things will change, get better, or divine intervention might intervene on our behalf. So most of us wait, and the day arrives when no choice is left. We are swept away in the flow of events swirling around us and during the decade of the 1960s, mighty indeed, were the storms of change.

So I set sail with the vague goal of exploration and I drifted, drifted without a destination, compass, or map to navigate fair winds, storms, or doldrums. Candide-like, I vowed to make the best of any situation and an indifferent universe accepted my challenge. Many a pirate, shipwreck and mermaid were to follow…

"The big question is whether you are going to be able to say a hearty yes to your adventure."
Joseph Campbell

THE HERO'S JOURNEY IN FOUR EASY STEPS

I

Fantasy Island
Malibu, CA
1965

"What are you, some kind of math whiz?" He had my test scores in his hand.

"No Sir. I was an English major."

"Good. Then you can read as well as think. Better than some, we got around here. We'll start you sorting mail. That's the usual entry-level position for new hires. Welcome to the Malibu Post Office. You begin Monday at seven thirty."

Malibu! Surf. Women. Beach. Women. Somehow, I had stumbled into Paradise riding the wave of a simple aptitude test for employment with the U.S. Post Office. Twenty-two years old and a town full of rich divorcees, parties, and world-famous surfing.

I went back to the apartment to share the good news with my roommate, Charlie. A note on the coffee table said the Red Cottage had called him in for a shift tending bar.

Man, we had it made now, chicks at the bar, and soon me delivering mail to bored housewives.

Under his note, our own mail lay next to Sports Illustrated and Surfer magazines. An official looking envelop had my name. I picked it up and tore off the end. I unfolded the document and the Earth stood still. "Greetings from the President of the United ……"

Shit! A draft notice requiring me to go downtown for a physical. Why did I skip a semester at Santa Monica Community College? I could get married. No. That would be worse than the Army. Flunk the physical? Impossible. The Army? How ordinary. What could I do? Conscientious objector! No chance. I hadn't been to church since my junior high school girlfriend Glenda and her family moved to San Francisco.

I opened the fridge and gabbed one of Charlie's beers. Wasn't there some kind of war going on? The Army could be dangerous. The TV stood there like a drug inviting me to escape. I pushed the power button.

My favorite program as a kid jumped up: The Silent Service. Submarines. That Elite Brotherhood of unique and gifted danger seekers who could always submerge and escape just before, well, danger. Yes! What a brilliant idea! Join the Navy!

So, I did.

A month later, Bob McGurk and I swore the oath of allegiance to the Constitution and the US Navy Reserve. Once again, I had beaten the system and postponed any real inconvenience by sacrificing only one weekend a month. Drinking coffee, hanging out with other guys in costumes, and sitting through classes on military etiquette was actually fun.

Bob got caught with painted eyeballs on his eyelids. From the back row it appeared to the instructor, he was wide-awake and alert. All went well until a hot summer day when Bob started snoring. Exemplary sidekick that he was, he never told the Chief Petty Officer it was my idea.

We attended Submarine School at Hunters Point for two months. Kinda like boarding school but if old enough, students could grab a beer on base after classes. Those of us finishing in the top percentile, qualified to go on a daylong diesel submarine cruise. A week later, just outside the Golden Gate Bridge with six students aboard, our Captain dove the boat.

Loud ooaguuuugah honked, bells rang and compartments turned deep red. I kept drinking coffee with the radioman in his coffin-like shack and leaned against the bulkhead. The boat put an angle on the bow and down we went. Just like on TV.

Then, it happened.

The whole boat shuddered like we hit the bottom of the bay. Alarms went off with terrifying tones. Smoke floated up out of the forward sections. The crew yelled and turned dials, others slammed watertight doors sealing us in small metal boxes. I squeezed my coffee cup tighter. Maybe the Army wasn't such a bad idea after all. Out of the corner of my eye. I saw the radio operator calmly reading a girlie magazine. Hmmmmmm....

After docking back at Hunters Point, our training officer debriefed the four of us left. "You can see that two of your classmates are no longer with us. They have been transferred to the Surface Skimmer Fleet. Do you know why?"

The other three guys were looking at me. I raised my hand. "Sir, was it because they were screaming and crying?" Like a brave sailor. I didn't smile.

The Lt. Commander shot me his "I'll talk to you later" look.

"That's correct, Seaman. The drill is standard procedure to fabricate a crisis, in this case a collision. We evaluate your performance in class and compare it to how you respond to a crisis while submerged. The four of you are now Submariners. Congratulations. You are now qualified to sail with the Navy's finest."

That autumn I attended UC Berkeley and transferred reserve meetings to Alameda Naval Station. My active duty obligation was a year away. I found a job at local drug store delivering menstrual products to sororities and my pal John moved in to celebrate our own version of the Free Speech Movement. All went well until I met a beautiful anti-war protester, Idell Wedemeyer.

II
Human Sacrifice
Berkeley, CA
1965

Flag? Country? Tradition? Ethical and moral position? No. It was the great body of Idell Wedemeyer that led me to protest an illegal and immoral police action in a far-away country posing no threat to the United States. It all happened in one wonderful night...

"Here, try some of this." A smile to die for.

"Idell, I can't get stoned. This is a Reserve weekend and I gotta get up early to go to Alameda."

She rubbed a perky breast against me and cooed, "And you look so cute in your uniform. The organizing committee and I were hoping you'd join us on the protest march tomorrow. We can walk together and you'll wear your uniform! It would make such a statement. I would be soooooo grateful."

Those eyes! What the hell. I could miss one meeting. I took a hit and we left the others scheming high drama and adjourned to her bedroom.

"Time to get up, my love. After the march well come right back here and celebrate."

Oh Boy! A naked angel hovered above promising a return to Paradise. Hand in hand, we strolled over to my apartment on Dwight Way. I dressed in Navy Blues and we walked one block to Telegraph Avenue where the march was forming up. Two miles later, we were to gather in the central park for speeches, folk singers, and lots of booing.

A guy dressed like Abraham Lincoln approached. "You did it Idell! You must be Brent. Welcome. We are proud to have the first military man with the courage to join brothers and sisters in the movement to bring an end to this terrible and unjust war."

Did he always talk like that? Idell wove her arm through mine. "We are going to be in the front line. Just like in Vietnam!"

What the fuck did I get myself into this time? Well, for a while everything went well: lots of posters, chanting, noisemakers, and liberal women. Then, we crossed the Oakland border. All the joy, flowers, and cheers of spectators faded away. Only poor residents with no jobs, no community activities, or money to go shopping lined the sidewalks. Marchers drew in tighter and our circus quieted down.

We approached the intersection of Ashby Avenue and heard catcalls, insults, yelling, and booing as the public protested protesters. What a party. We started yelling back.

In a flash of blue, my worst nightmare came true. The Alameda Naval Reserve unit on lunch break stretched half way down the block. In addition to being AWOL, participating in a public protest in a military uniform was a federal offense. Now, sex with Free Speech Movement women was great, but peeling potatoes for six months on punitive sea duty seemed to be quite a price to pay.

I let go of Idell's arm, stood still and buried myself within the human stream of marchers flowing pass me. Time enough to figure a way out and disappear.

"Hey, asshole!" The Southern twang of Chief Petty Officer Jefferson ran through the parade like a torpedo at thirty knots. Stupidly, I looked back along the sonar path and made eye contact. What to do?

I ran. Ran back through the parade and at the next corner, ran right (starboard actually). All traffic had been re-routed, and appearing there before me, the yellow dye maker on a stormy sea: a cab.

Back at our apartment, John suggested we have a drink. "What are you going to do?"

Sympathetic and supportive, my roommate did not want to be accessory after the fact by suggesting an escape route. I finished dressing in civvies and considered the right thing to do.

"They still have to get back to Alameda before they notify the Provost Marshall. I'm leaving Berkeley right now." He didn't want to know more than that. I grabbed my backpack, fled to the airport and returned to Los Angeles.

My brother-in-law, George, picked me up at the LA Airport. "You look like shit. Here, take a hit of this hash. Still one step ahead of disaster as usual, I see." A part-time criminal, ironworker, and rascal extraordinaire, George did not judge others.

"I'm fucked now, George. I called John and he said the Shore Patrol showed up fifteen minutes after I left."

"Well, Little Bro. I been thinking this one over. Other than the brig or a life on the run, there is only one other choice." He exhaled and waved at a motorcycle cop as we left the airport. The cop waved back. George had a gift.

"You can transfer immediately to another branch of service for immediate active duty. With the war going on and the draft pickin up everybody for cannon fodder, it should be a piece of cake. Plus it fits in with your career of movin on to the next thing."

He laughed his great laugh and we stopped at the next liquor store for a case of beer. The next morning, I walked into the Marine Corps recruiting station.

"You have it made in Submarines. If you sign this you will go to boot camp, infantry training, and directly to Vietnam."

How refreshing, a compassionate NCO. "Thanks for telling me the truth. Just want to do the right thing, Sergeant."

Guess my arrest warrant had yet to circulate inter-service. Oh well. Life was nothing but a joke anyway. Plus, I had to stay true to my Code of The Next Thing. I was clever, quick, and charming. How bad could it be?

III
Patriot
San Diego, CA
1966

"Jesus Christ! You were a fuckin' Swabby?!"

My Marine Corps drill instructor didn't seem very impressed. Why the reaction? I was already a fellow service member, kinda. Of course in old war movies the Navy and Marines were always fighting each other while on weekend passes but I thought he was taking this little incident a bit too far. Little did I know that the Marines were actually a part of the Navy and the taunts, teasing, and trauma resulted in two centuries of broken bones.

True, Sergeant Butler had to take fifteen minutes off from abusing our boot camp platoon and march me down to the base post office for registered mail. There might be a joint, a six-pack of beer, or some wire cutters to escape through the wire fences of our Marine Corps Recruit Depot. If only it had been a simple felony.

Instead, there in his little hand was an impressive, suitable-for-framing, document in glittering gold letters:
Honorable Discharge
United States Navy

Butler jammed my discharge into his mail pouch, "About turn, Swabby!" and marched me over to the maintenance shed.

"Get eight mops you college bag of puke! Stack "em at port arms on your shoulder."

Now what? Even though his only talent was puffing up his chest, he did have moments of demented inspiration.

"Attention! We are going to stop at every platoon's Quonset hut. You will place a mop at the font door. Salute it. You will sing your fuckin Swabby hymn at the top of your shit-filled lungs. Do you understand me?"

I almost said. 'Aye Aye. Sir.' But that would have sent him deeper into his psychotic episode

"Sir. Yes Sir!"

And off we went. Maybe three huts later my mentor realized that I enjoyed singing and was having a good time. Off to the obstacle course where I ran laps with the remaining mops (swabs in military vernacular) until I puked.

As a reminder that I was indeed a retard. I swabbed the Drill Instructor's hut for the remaining weeks of boot camp. Even now. every time I puke. I think of Sergeant Butler.

IV
Return of the Naïve
Berkeley, CA
1966

For reasons unknown to me, Good Sergeant and Bad Sergeant (Butler) promoted me out of boot camp. As the resident college bag of puke, I taught English to Native Americans, Mexicans, and ex cons. (Actually, we memorized the exit test). Every recruit graduated and got infantry except the most Gung Ho kid, who played saxophone. He went to the USMC Band. He cried. Really.

With a tight-fitting green uniform, in tiptop shape, and with a silver sharp shooter medal, I was ready for some civilian drama. After a few days of visiting buddies, beer drinking, and strutting around, I reflected on how best to utilize my new persona, The Proud, The Few: United States Marine

Just what had I learned? Marching. Yes, that was it! Now that I had mastered the art form, why not return to Berkeley and show the rebel scum (and impress beautiful Idell) just how to march and have some fun too?

Yes. Walk down Telegraph Avenue in the opposite direction: from the Oakland border to the UC campus, brush away the rabble of beggars, street vendors, and posers with a puffed-up chest and a few well-rehearsed lines. My hole card? I could now mimic the Evil Eye of Sergeant Butler.

And a few nights later, that's just what I did.

Strange how an image, symbol, or in my case a uniform created a knee jerk reaction in a given community. The language of the liberal and compassionate street people matched that of my mentor, Sergeant Butler. There I was, wrapped in a garment, the same guy who had marched in the opposite direction just months ago in a different military uniform, memorialized by the anti-war movement as a temporary hero and Sacrificial Lamb.

Enough philosophy, time to focus on the mission, Idell. If only the rabble knew that I was on my way to make Love, not War.

"Is Idell home?" What was Abraham Lincoln doing there?

"Idell! Come check this out!"

Emerging from her bedroom, the angel of my dreams entered the living room, this time with more of her to love. I stared at her stomach.

"Don't worry, I was pregnant when we recruited you. What are you doing in that uniform? We all thought you went to Canada. Want to get stoned?"

Recruited? Jesus! If you can't trust radicals to have some sort of espirit de corps, and honor, who can you?

I was to find out shortly.

"What are they gonna do? Send me to Vietnam?"
Response of Vietnam bound troops
contemplating a questionable act

The Three Wise Men
Defense Language Institute
Monterey, CA
Fall, 1966

The graduation party was going well; Chinese food for eighteen in downtown Monterey, California at the Golden Duck Palace. Our officer in charge, whom we called Lieutenant Numbnuts, stood and assumed credit for our academic achievements through his due diligence and motivation. Someday, studying with the U.S. Army would be remembered as the easiest tour of duty serving with the Marine Corps.

We had arrived four months earlier on a Greyhound bus from Camp Pendleton, four hours before our transit orders expired at midnight. Ten Marines stood on the sidewalk with ten duffle bags at 8 PM in a tourist town. What to do? As senior enlisted man by a week, I ordered the squad to shoulder bags and to march in formation to the nearest bar.

We found a circular glassed-in pub overlooking the yacht harbor. With instincts that served me well in combat, I scouted out two retired Marines sitting in a booth. They waved us over and bought all the drinks. Time passed.

Three minutes before midnight, we poured out of taxis at the top of Presidio Hill and reported to a sleepy Army sergeant. Drunk and rowdy had little impact on late-night security, for the only other Marines of his acquaintance must have served in WWII movies. Apparently, we matched the stereotype.

Early next morning after roll call, our designated Officer In Charge, Lt. Numbnuts, roostered an inspirational speech. "Your aptitude scores indicate you are the best Camp Pendleton has to offer at this time. Obviously, you can acquire Vietnamese in four months and if you do not, it means you are a shitbird and will be prosecuted for dereliction of duty. Not go get some chow and don't embarrass me or you will regret it."

Yes, guinea pig Marines. If we successfully demonstrated enlisted Marines could actually learn, (an issue much discussed by the other armed services) more and larger groups would follow.

We soon learned the Army really did know how to motivate! Six classes, six hours a day, six days a week, taught by young, attractive Vietnamese women. Pride in early progress faded when Army pals at the Enlisted Club revealed our teachers feared failure. As Vietnamese nationals, their administrator would lose face and return them not only to a far less privileged life-style back home but to civil war. No one ever failed a test in their classes - or gotten laid. (Everyone holding out for an officer - no doubt).

Our graduation party needed lubrication. Two bottles of Orange Flavored Eden Roc set me back almost five bucks.

"Give me some of that wine you got under the table, Mac."

"OK, but give Ron some."

"Of course, Dipshit."

My fellow wine connoisseurs from South Texas knew the vintage well. Using evasion tactics learned during infantry training, our three Chinese teacups moved back and forth under the tablecloth like a boat of refugees escaping under the cover of darkness.

The crinkling of paper bags went unnoticed amidst laughter and conversation around the banquet table. Still seated inside the Golden Duck Palace, the three of us were soon transported to Eden and my natural leadership qualities surfaced despite a year of military discipline.

Graduation would spilt-up our holy trinity. The first group of ten Marines sent to the famous Defense Language Institute in Monterey, CA, graduated! Had we enlisted Marines performed at this sophisticated level? No one really knew. Five of our group and their twangy South Texas accents butchered the tonal Vietnamese language. For the instructors it was either give Jimmy a passing score or get on a plane and fly 9,000 miles to the war zone with him. War is Hell.

Jimmy got a C-. Once in country he and the other Texans were reassigned as grunts where their grunting of

Vietnamese did not alienate the hearts and minds of local villagers. Yes, we had all passed and not burned the place down. Something had to be done!

I turned away from flirting with the cuter female teachers and scouted for a Chinese target. A souvenir perhaps? Under the pretense of complementing the cooks, I left the table and pushed through swinging double doors to the kitchen. Jimmy followed along and behind him the manager, wringing his hands. Fuck it. What were they going to do? Send me to Vietnam? This war cry preceded stateside acts of bravery often requiring disciplinary action.

I chatted up the cooks while circling the kitchen and scanned the kitchen utensils hanging on the wall for a possible candidate. Of course! There, shining and glittering, calling out to me, the classical weapon of choice for a warrior: a meat cleaver!

"Jimmy, distraction."

We had faced similar challenges. Magically, a plate of food fell off the prep table and crashed on the tile floor. As a highly trained guerilla fighter, I smoothly slid the cleaver under my tunic and walked back to the banquet room while Jimmy took the Chinese heat.

Still high on vitamin C and with orange tongues from our wine, Ron, Jimmy, and I climbed up Presidio Hill to the dormitory. Just as on our first night, the midnight bell from the old Spanish mission echoed from in the town below. Reaching the top, we saw it. A cardboard Nativity scene stood on the grassy knoll by the rear entrance to the

18

dorm stood. Spotlights stuck in the grass highlighted three figures looming over an unsuspecting family. Wise men, like three opportunistic colonels, stood gazing down at the new draftee in a manger. Joe and Mary looked ready to sign consent papers for enlistment.

Roly-poly Jesus, a three-dimensional white plastic Pillsbury Dough Boy, smiled up at us with his extended umbilical cord running twenty feet to an electrical outlet. Inside his tummy, a light bulb illuminated and expanded his aura into the night and holiday season.

Poor guy. Jesus was to suffer the same fate as four Marines from our class, but while they fell in obscure forests and jungles, Jesus suffered through the most publicized public execution recorded. As a Marine, I couldn't leave him behind.

With prophetic foresight, the mission became crystal clear. The meat cleaver. An instant later, the heads of the Three Colonels lay on the ground, no longer a threat to the underage recruit.

"Jesus Christ, Mac!" Ron was Catholic.

"Exactly. Unplug that extension cord." I grabbed Jesus and stuck him in the huge doggie bag we hauled all the way back from the restaurant, the manager glad to get rid of us.

"Let's go."

"No shit." Jimmy now fired only one or two words in burst. Trained as a machine gunner, he saved his ammo.

Back at the dorm room, our overachiever, Ron, paced back and forth. "Holy shit. They'll know its us. They'll search our rooms and I'll get busted."

I already lost a stripe for coming in late and a bit tipsy, (and getting caught), so I reassured him. "It doesn't hurt."

"Put him back! There's still time before the MPs do the 0200 check."

We still held Jesus. This seemed too good an opportunity to waste. "OK, you go back to your room. I swear He will return to the manger in a few minutes."

I pondered. What would Jesus do to a guy who embraced all mankind? Ah, yes. Thanks to Eden Roc Winery and the Marine Corps with men and women from every ethnic group in America, my own light bulb lit up.

The cafeteria next morning buzzed and hummed like a beehive with overdressed bees. The few black brothers eating in the corner together seemed particularly animated.

Lt. Numbnuts separated from his little group of the officer elite and marched over, no doubt to wish us bon voyage and well done.

A hand on his hip was one of his favorite poses. "What time did you Shitbirds sign in last night?

Ron had the most practice at playing it straight. "The Sarge was asleep at the desk with his head down on the clip board, so we just went on up."

I got the feeling he didn't believe us and I didn't look up from Snap, Crackle, and Pop in the cereal bowl.

His official leadership voice barked. "Some asshole vandalized the nativity scene last night. He painted shoe black on the face and extremities of Baby Jesus and plugged him back in. We're lucky it didn't start a riot. I want to inspect all your rooms immediately after breakfast!"

He did a clumsy about-face and marched off to his social equals.

Ron rubbed the newly awarded stripe on his shoulder. "Jesus, Mac."

"Exactly."

PART TWO

In Vietnam, the first few weeks passed with little enemy contact. Surrounded by characters, costumes and the special effects of wartime. I continued playing at "warrior". An occasional booby trap, sniper or rocket kept us alert and along with other new arrivals, I started to believe that it wasn't so bad after all. This was soon to change...

March 1967: Quang Nam Province caught fire. People began to die with regularity and the fog of my existential relativity evaporated. Both terrifying and exhilarating, the world around me shifted into colored-coded, black and white. Enemy tried to kill us and we tried to kill them. No confusion, no bullshit, no speculation.

The official KIA list for Foxtrot Company holds one-hundred-sixty dead, the equivalent of two wartime infantry companies. Failure to pay attention and behave properly resulted in death for one's self and frequently, others. We lived a violent utopia of co-dependency and brotherhood. Petty differences such as race, education, and rank dissolved with the first incoming round. My need to belong to a community sharing the same consciousness, cooperation and commitment had arrived with a high price tag.

Yet, Hemmingway still haunted me. Like a bullfighter facing the moment of truth, I had yet to experience epiphany in that second before death, that flash of illumination in which the secret of the Great Mystery is revealed. On June 2, 1967 the crack in the universe opened and answered my unspoken prayer.

Operation Union II, from May 15 to June 5th, 1967, is documented as one of the bloodiest battles in the long years of war and in the late afternoon of June 2nd, a U-shaped ambush decimated Foxtrot. I lay face down in a dry rice paddy, alone and unarmed, while a machine gun sprayed rounds back and forth. A burning red tracer round stuck in a dirt clod in front of my nose, gradually fizzled out and turned black. "The Moment" had arrived. I waited for revelation. Nothing.

Now what? Try a prayer? - OK.

"Dear, Whoever or Whatever. I don't want anything but if there is something going on that I don't know about, would you give me a little sign? Maybe a lightening bolt or something"?"

Nothing. Bullets kept coming.

Then I understood. This moment is all there is, full of Life It Self, every human possibility and choice. As I received this obvious and tardy insight, the enemy stopped firing. Happy, transformed. I wanted for the first time in memory, to live, live fully.

But there I was, face down in a rice paddy, alone, and in the midst of chaos and carnage. Now what?

*"Behold, how good and how pleasant it is
for Brethren to dwell together in unity."*
Psalms 133:1

Vietnamese Playboy
An Hoa, Vietnam
1967

In the first week of January, a C130 transport plane dumped me onto the red mud of An Hoa, Vietnam. The 2nd Battalion of the 5th Marine Regiment ran patrols and sweeps into "Indian Country" and rotated one infantry company each month to stand security on top of Nong Son Mountain, four miles away.

Excited and nervous, I stood at attention in front of the Battalion First Sergeant ready for assignment as a specialist in interrogation or intelligence. He shuffled through my file for a few seconds and handed it back to me.

"OK Private, go on over to Fox Company. They need riflemen."

A grunt? A common rifleman? I didn't move.

He turned back to the tall stack of paper on his desk. Overworked and worn out, he stared up at me. "What are you waiting for Private?"

"First Sergeant, I don't know if you noticed but I attended Vietnamese language school."

He stood. "We don't need no fuckin' gook talkers. We need riflemen. Now get the fuck over there!"

As a new member of the 1st Platoon I kept my mouth shut and tried to learn from more experienced grunts how to survive. After weeks of patrols, ambushes, sand bagging, operations, and sleep deprivation - Hugh Hefner intervened on my behalf.

Local Vietnamese militia officers invited our company commander to meet and discuss collaboration at a local village. A few days later, Fox Company encircled the selected site and as I walked by with my squad, the gunny pulled two of us out to stand guard duty in front of a grass hut.

Gunny Jones grumbled. "Keep your shit together. The Colonel's comin over from An Hoa for the meeting inside. Don't fuck up!"

Me and Rabbi shrugged and assumed what we thought to be intimidating foreign devil personas on each side of the door. Time passed so we started bullshitting and relaxed. Villagers noticed we had dissolved into human beings and curious, approached.

"Rabbi, watch this. I'll blow their minds."

I turned and faced the dozen or so villagers. "Chao Cac Ong. Manh gioi?" (Howdy everybody. How are you?)

The crowd laughed and moved closer. A foreign devil spoke Vietnamese, and with a terrible and comical accent.

Rabbi stiffened. "Jesus, Mac! What the fuck did you say?"

"Shalom."

"Well, tell em to move back! What's that guy in the back pullin out?" Rabbi released the safety on his M14.

"Lai dei!" I called the man forward.

"It's a Playboy magazine, Rabbi."

The villager opened his magazine and showed me a full-page cartoon. "Cai nai la yi?" (What is this?)

It took five minutes to explain the cultural concept of pictorial humor. In an effort to win hearts and minds, I began a presentation of the Playboy jokes. Soon, thirty villagers gathered in front of us laughing and howling as I translated captions.

"What the hell is going on here?"

Rabbi and I snapped to attention. Our Colonel came around from behind the hut with his bodyguards.

"Uh, Sir. I was just translating these Playboy jokes for the folks here, Sir."

"How the hell do you speak Vietnamese, son?"

"Sir, I attended DLI in Monterey."

"What's your job with Foxtrot, Private?"

"Rifleman, Sir."

"Come with me."

We entered the darkened hut with six allied officers sitting on the ground.

The Colonel interrupted, "Captain Graham, did you know this Marine speaks Vietnamese and is assigned as a rifleman in your company? If you don't use him appropriately. I will take him back with me to Battalion."

"Colonel. I didn't know. We'll bring him into the CP as an interpreter."

"Damn right you will. Now introduce me to our new friends here." He grabbed my arm. "Son, you sit next to me and make sure they don't bullshit us."

"Yes, Sir."

As the source of his discomfort. I tried not to look at Captain Graham. My life had just changed forever and thanks to the universal appeal of Playboy Magazine. I was to return home. Ist Platoon suffered was to suffer many casualties.

"One man with courage makes a majority."

Saying

Gladiator
Battle of Union II, Vietnam
June 2, 1967

I transferred to the small CP (Command Personnel) as company radioman, translator, and as ordered by the Gunny, to trade my life for Captain Graham's if necessary: I was "replaceable". During the daylight hours and until the day he died on June 2, I was his constant companion, shadow, and relay voice to our platoons and weapons people. We came to know each other well.

My first impression of Jim Graham was one of mental instability. His enthusiasm for combat was child-like, yet his physical appearance was intense, lean, and hungry. Some predator caged in the same body had escaped into his own personal hunting ground: Vietnam. A large hooked nose dominated his features. He often reminded me of a hawk.

He was one of the rare ones, thriving in the most difficult of circumstances, spirit soaring, senses electric, and dancing skillfully with the shadow of death hovering above An Hoa. Most of us in Foxtrot Company just wanted to go home.

The Captain looked much older than his 27 years. He had a serious demeanor yet practiced a compassionate humor with everyone and enjoyed an especially had a good rapport with fellow officers and NCO staff. Respected, courageous, and popular, he continuously studied situation reports, maps, personnel, and reviews of intelligence flowing from various sources. He was, as the saying goes, "Born Ready."

We all felt he was the best possible commander in the most difficult of times. An aggressive and tactical leader, he enabled Foxtrot to gain a few victories in the midst of chaos and attrition. We had pride in our company and ourselves.

At the time, it appeared that Captain Graham's personal mission was not the promotion ladder. For him, combat was the opportunity of a lifetime: Field Commander. He lusted after contact, engagement, battle, and all this he pursued at every chance. My single reservation? I felt he believed that he had been anointed to embrace a special destiny, and this would one day lead us to destruction. It was not ambition per se but a powerful inner force which others felt and interpreted each in our own way.

I respected Captain Graham's obsessive habits as these made all of us better warriors. He inspired confidence. We saw other companies come and go, and suffer casualties through horrendous mistakes. He was disciplined both professionally and privately.

He carried a Bible and toilet articles in the field when no one else did. He changed fatigues in the middle of nowhere. We were grungy. He washed, shaved, brushed his teeth, and put on pressed fatigues; always ready and at his best.

In those days, I saw him as an archetype, living out an almost missionary vision. Each day he put on his robes, made his absolution, and said his prayers. He was, I felt, ready to die at all times. This impression, I later came to understand in later years was of a man fully prepared to live and function in the present moment.

Yet all around him, we enlisted men felt the war was a sham and not worth dying for. I feared Graham would one day lead us into the Valley of Death for absolutely no reason.

That day finally arrived on June 2, 1967. A long, dry rice paddy lay before us and a ripple of apprehension traveled through the entire company. For the first time, I witnessed Graham hesitate and then question the order given to him by Colonel Hilgartner of 1/5 to advance. Our Captain had good reasons. There was evidence to suggest formidable enemy forces were waiting in the tree line across the paddy. And indeed, they were…

Captain Jim Graham *was* courageous when the time came; not with guns blazing to assault and destroy but in a doomed effort to save our people in the second platoon ambushed in the rice paddy. He was an authentic hero, a caring person who did the right thing at the right time and sacrificed himself in an impossible situation.

The last time I saw Jim Graham he laid dead on a poncho. He had given everything in the face of certain death. For me, our family died that day. Our Captain was gone and with him the heart and soul of Foxtrot. James Graham received the Congressional Medal of Honor posthumously.

"And that had he told them, they would have
answered with a shocked, uncomprehending stare."
Edward Fields, *Icarus*

The Walking Dead
An Hoa Base, Vietnam
June 5, 1967

I am a hollow statue wearing a skin of ragged uniform, gear, weapons and dirt. I have no body.

Floating in a bad dream, we few survivors climb down off the helicopters. Zombies in filthy fatigues, some partially clothed some in bandages, others dazed and supported by companions.

Impotent and armed only with a pencil, our Fox Company admin-clerk stands counting bodies as we stagger towards the double line of huts and hooches. His name? My mind is numb.

He recognizes me. "Mac!"

I keep moving, going - somewhere.

His lips move again. "Johnson?"

I shake my head.

"Driscoll? The mortar squad?"

A voice moves through me, whispers. "No."

I keep moving. Our hooch looks a thousand meters away and in the same moment, I feel wooden steps under my feet. The screen door squeaks as always, as though nothing has happened. Inside the silent space, cots and footlockers stand squared away, waiting for their Marines.

Lying on his stolen bookshelf are Joe's phonograph and pirated record albums from R&R in Bangkok. New letters from Driscoll's mom scatter across his rack. Sarge's collection of *Popular Mechanics*, remains stacked under his cot. Next to Mike's pillow, a pencil pokes out, leading to his notebook of poetry.

Our hooch stands ready for their return, faithful and intimate possessions waiting to be brought to life again by human touch. Now these things too are dead, tombstones in a graveyard full of ghosts. Rows of cots like empty coffins await bodies they once comforted. Every one dead. Everyone, but me.

Someone moves off to my left. Who violates this holy ground? With a hand on my pistol and the Evil Eye, I turn and stare down the stranger. An old man, filthy, bearded, with dead eyes stares back.

I confront him. "What the fuck are you look…"

His mouth is open. He moves as I move. I am yelling, challenging a mirror. A stranger. What happened to - *me*? The person I remember just a few days ago is no more.

The old man stares back and I see in his eyes a part of me, lying out in that rice paddy in a body bag. I sit down on the end of my cot. I want to cry, need to cry. But there are no tears in this grey shadow land I have entered into.

But I know now: I will survive. They can't kill a ghost.

"They use their instinctive sense of observation to help others in times of need and are among the most fit of all the Animal signs to survive most any situation."
The Rat
Chinese Astrology

Man's Best Friend
Phu Loc 6 Outpost, Vietnam
1967

"Mac, you sleep in the communication bunker tonight and man both radios. Cowboy is out on ambush."

"Gunny, he told me there's a big rat in there that runs around in the dark."

"Just leave a couple of C Ration cans open near the entrance when you hit the rack. We got him trained."

"OK."

Two radios stood on top of some wooden crates in the corner, and above a light bulb dangled down from bare wires hooked up to a jeep battery. Rows of leaky sandbags dribbled streams of sand with every vibration echo from 80-millimeter mortars firing illumination rounds for the patrols down by the river. Spooky. Like the inside of a large intestine with ulcers bleeding sand.

I threw my pack on top of the cot and sat on three ammo cans stacked in front of the radios. Gunny bent down and stuck his head through the doorway. "You can sleep after 2400 but turn the volume up and wear headphones."

"What's the name of the operation tomorrow?"

"Dixie. You are on the first APC[*] with the radio. Should be routine. Red will be here at 0600 to brief you on secure frequencies and codes."

"Where we goin?'"

"Across the river and through all the villes. Show of force." He turned and spit tobacco juice on the red soil. "Scare the shit out of 'em."

"OK, Gunny."

Life as company radioman kept me in the flow of info. As part of the CP* and surrounded by three platoons of riflemen, we only engaged the enemy in moments of chaos and imminent disaster. A much better job than my previous role as rifleman where the source of information was megaphone barking by Sgt. Henderson.

On Dixie, my radio and I would ride on top of a motorized personnel carrier, call in observations, and pass along communications. The best part? Yelling down at former squad members, ground pounding through red mud.

Around 1900 hours I got hungry. Under the moldy cot, empty boxes of C-rats competed for space with a new case of gourmet-cuisine-in-a can. I bent down to make my selection. The top of the case was gone, along with every box except one last, "Beans and Wieners." Someone had looted the contents and no doubt traded it down in the ville for contraband or pussy.

---

[*] APC = Armored Personnel Carrier.

When you're hungry, even cold franks and beans taste good. Special packets of cheese and crackers, a mini chocolate bar, and everyone's favorite pound cake, and cold instant coffee, topped off the feast.

Ten minutes later, I wired the empty cans together in the doorway as an alarm. Sappers had penetrated the smaller outpost down the road some weeks before, and everyone was more paranoid than usual.

Cardboard on top of the ammo can chair softened my butt as patrols called in from checkpoints every fifteen minutes. After midnight, they set up ambush scenarios and radio silence followed until dawn or until the shit hit the fan. I spun the dial looking for Vietnamese radio conversations and chipped in with some juicy swear words learned from our Vietnamese scouts. The gooks went ape shit. Sometimes out of boredom, I called our own platoon radiomen and spoke Vietnamese just to mind-fuck 'em. Gotta keep 'em alert, you know.

Midnight came around and I unscrewed the light bulb, grabbed the headphones, and got comfy on the cot. The occasional popping of illumination flares, random gunshots, and the hum of high-level aircraft serenaded me to sleep…

In my dream, Glenda and I danced the last dance at our high school prom. We melted together, each holding the promise of a sweet night to follow. Someone tapped my arm trying to cut in. I ignored him. Probably that asshole, Algie with the red Plymouth Fury convertible. He tapped again, harder. I held Glenda tighter. Pain. A knife pierced my left bicep and I screamed!

Back in the bunker, someone had hold of my bicep with a pair of pliers and twisted. I reached across to beat him off with my fist and pounded into fur. The bunker rat wouldn't let go, so I pulled my pistol from its holster and started pounding.

He finally scurried away, no doubt to rejoin his communist trainer. Alarm cans rattled and a flashlight beam speared me from the open doorway.

"What the fuck's goin on in here? You got the whole perimeter on lock and load!"

"It was the rat, Gunny. He took a chunk out of my arm. I left the cans out like you said." His light moved down and tracked the empty cans on the wire.

"Dipshit! You're supposed to leave food in the damn cans! He bit you 'cause he's pissed. Just like me! Now I gotta send you back to Battalion for rabies shots. How the fuck am I gonna train another radioman in three fuckin' hours?"

"I'll do it."

"Damn right you will. I'll send Doc over to stop that bleeding and get someone from 2nd Platoon for the radio. Don't fuck up."

"Yes, Gunny." (The guy loved me.)

The light bulb lit up the bunker again. I wrapped a rag around my bicep and set up the radios for a lesson. I felt someone behind me and I turned to see a skinny kid standing under a helmet. He looked about twelve.

"Come on in and pull up an ammo can. What's your name?

"Bobby Jackson. I came in with the replacements last week. Went to com school back in Pendleton, so Gunny sent me over. Sorry about your bite. Think you'll get a Purple Heart?"

He learned everything I could teach in about ten minutes so I let him play with the frequencies, dial up radio watch back at Battalion, and talk radio talk. Bright kid.

Doc came and I spent the last few hours before dawn in his tent. Right on schedule, two APCs roared up just after sunrise. Jackson crawled up on top of the first one with our flamethrower team, smiling all the while like he was off to summer camp.

I yelled up, "Don't trash my lucky radio, Jackson. Took a month to get a new battery."

"OK, Mac." Jesus. In daylight, I could see he had buckteeth.

A convoy with two platoons of grunts and the APCs left through the opening in the concertina wire and rumbled off down the road heading for the river.

"Mac! Get your shit and jump on the resupply chopper when it turns around. Two weeks goofin' off back there with rear shit birds. Hope they make you burn the shit."

"Yes, Gunny."

Fourteen rabies shots had a bad reputation. But new a vaccine injected subcutaneously didn't torture as advertised. Gunny would be disappointed. Since I had to report to the hospital shed every day, my rear job as gopher for the doctors went smoothly until the second day.

Three medivac choppers landed on the helipad carrying casualties from Operation Dixie. Overhead, two other copters flew east in the direction of graves registration.

"Grab a gurney and follow me!" Colonel Viti lead the way.

First off was a burn victim from the flamethrower team. Doc Viti shot him up with morphine until the screaming stopped. Hard to tell with the burns and all, but he looked like Tony from the flame team.

"Tony. Its me, Mac. What happened?"

Through groans and tears, he told the story. "Our APC hit a mine and the diesel fuel tank exploded. Blew me into the river. The rest of them didn't make it. Only me."

He passed out.

Viti yelled at the chopper pilot through the cockpit side window. "Got enough fuel for Da Nang? OK. Take this guy to MAC5 trauma unit."

We loaded Tony back on the H34, watched it lift off and fly east towards the coast. The rat bite started to burn. I rubbed my arm and started thinking how things play out.

Much has changed in the last forty-two years since Vietnam. I still haven't figured out much. Shit happens, or

41

doesn't. Bobby Jackson never made it to nineteen, and part of me never made it home. But each year on the night before Memorial Day, I open up a can of gourmet beef, leave it on the back porch, and salute Brother Rat. In the morning... it's all gone.

"Then up spoke Velleius, with all the confidence of men of his school, as if He himself just returned to Earth from some council of the gods."
The Nature of the Gods
Cicero, 50 B.C.

Major Principal
An Hoa, Vietnam
1967

All institutions with vertical staffing structure have much in common. Personality archetypes inhabiting various corporations are often interchangeable. Remember your junior high school vice principal? You know, the anal-retentive character primarily interested in the principle of vice and law enforcement. This guy patrolled the school grounds looking for the unsuspecting miscreant who tossed a bag lunch into the trash can after the latest regulation posted two minutes prior:

> "As of noon today all trash in the cafeteria area must be walked to the nearest trash can and dropped into the container. Throwing paper bags, milk cartons, etc. results in trash on the floor and more work for our maintenance staff."

> Mr. Walcott
> Vice Principal

Our guy matched the career profile of vice principals throughout the Los Angeles Unified School District: "Must be incompetent in the classroom, not qualified for promotion to principal, and by nature extremely unpopular with students and faculty." As Mr. Walcott patrolled the campus, the bravest of us boys would call out from the corner of a building "Get a real job, Wally!" and take off running.

So it is in the military. When the promotion board identifies an individual as having attained the highest level of incompetence, the candidate plateaus, or becomes "stuck" unless of course wartime necessitates promotion, for everyone else is dead, wounded, or noticeably crazy.

A Buddhist now, I often wonder if Mr. Walcott died in 1966 as a victim of Post Traumatic Stress Disorder brought on by his daily war with pubescent teenagers. Why? In the spring of 1967 I met him again reincarnated as Major Esau, a wanna-be colonel and assistant to the commander of the 2nd Battalion 5th Marine Regiment in An Hoa, Vietnam.

Yes, we too had trashcans in the combat zone. Next to every hooch, a receptacle held C-ration cans and boxes, exhausted toiletry items, and Dear John letters. Yet no one marched about and demanded a tidy firebase. We were all heavily armed! But there were other opportunities for over-zealous enforcement of the many, and often incomprehensible regulations.

Each and every day was filled with tasks, patrols, work details, guard duty, maintenance, and all the unwritten details of fighting a war. In addition to regulations, our ever-present and constant companions were fatigue and never enough sleep. Under-manned fire teams, squads, platoons, and companies meant more work for everyone, all the time. When sleep came during assigned shifts, no one fully slept. The survival mechanism had become so finely tuned that like wild animals our bodies were at rest, but a newly developed sixth sense constantly monitored and scanned our immediate surroundings, ready at all times for flight or fight in an instant. And this, dear reader, is our story....

An Hoa was heavily defended and not vulnerable to direct ground assault. The perimeter held a series of interlocking bunkers and fighting holes. Usually two men rotated guard duty and took turns sleeping. When the situation demanded, one man held a position on the outer ring and another would relieve him from inside the base. And so it was every night in An Hoa. To be found asleep while on guard duty was a court martial offense with a severe penalty.

How to prove a sentry might be asleep? If his rifle could be removed or 'captured' then "asleep while on duty" was the only conclusion. And how to catch the overworked and sleep-deprived teenager? Who would voluntarily sneak around in the darkness in a combat zone trying to ambush his own people and write them up for a violation? Who had the leisure time, energy, and character required for just such a mission: approach paranoid and violent Marines from behind and steal their weapons?

Yes, our reincarnated vice principal, Major Esau, the protagonist living his own war movie, scoring promotion points wherever he went and boring we enlisted with a nonstop narration of the obvious.

An Hoa, like every remote base, had a cocoanut wireless, an instantaneous network of communications relaying gossip like a hysterical colony of bees. We were strung out, wired, and connected.

"You hear! We're going to Israel to help out. Egypt and the other Arabs invaded." "Hey! 1st platoon is getting three days of R&R at China Beach. What about us!"

And so it was one early morning while filling sandbags my PRC25 radio buzzed with an incoming message. I grabbed the phone off the battery pack and squeezed the button.

"That fuckin' you, Mac? Over."

"Roger, Rabbi."

"You ain't gonna fuckin believe what went down last night on perimeter."

"Another water buffalo get past Red and Andy?"

"No Man! This is way better. That asshole Esau was sneakin around again tryin to catch someone nodding off. Guess who he went up on?"

All of a sudden, I got that funny feeling. We were all a bit crazy by the summer of that year but one type of

Marine more easily 'adjusted' to the chaos and killing of combat: Puerto Ricans. Maybe it was their DNA or too many people on a small island. Who knew? But when the shit went down, we were lucky to have a Riqueno brother by our side.

I didn't want to spoil Rabbi's moment. "What happened?"

"That dicklick major tried to sneak up on Taco. It's pitch black and Taco's sittin' in front of his bunker, slumped over with his head down. But you know that mutha fucker ain't slept in ten months!"

"Roger that."

"So Major Dipshit creeps up on Taco like a real Marine on a real ambush and slowly reaches around Taco to take his M16."

"Let me guess."

"Shut up asshole! So everybody in An Hoa knows Taco carries his own blade and sleeps with it in his hand, everybody except Major Dicklick that is."

I stared out across our bulldozed no-mans-land and saw Major Esau's decapitated head rolling down the hill into the village below. Kids were playing soccer with it. Nah, it couldn't be that good.

"So Xxxxx puts his hand around the barrel, oh so quiet like. Boom! Taco whips back with his knife and it goes all the way into Dicklick's thigh. Taco is on top of him, pulls out the blade and is about to get to cuttin' when he hears the gook screamin in English. 'It's me! Major Xxxxx! Don't do it!"

There was laughter and static in my ear. "Everyone in Blue Sector on perimeter heard it!"

I sat down on the pile of sandbags and let the phone dangle on its cord down into the bunker. Revelation. Epiphany. Catharsis. Forget about the Domino Theory. The war finally made sense! Justice. Redemption. Karma. We the meek, the enlisted, had inherited this small piece of Earth.

That afternoon, smiling faces filled the hooches, bunkers, chow lines, and latrines. No one spoke. And for one day, one beautiful day, the righteous hand of serendipity stuck a blow for Justice.

I think about Vice Principal Wally and Major Dicklick now and then. Have they resigned their commissions and joined the ranks of just plain folk? Nah. There hanging on some study wall hang their degrees, plaques, testimonials, photographs of Marines whose names they never knew, and medals. (Did the major ever thank Taco for getting him his purple heart?) All this memorabilia conjures up a man who then, like now, lives only in his imagination.

*"Music is one of the ways we can achieve a kind
of shorthand to understand each other."*
"Music"
Yo Yo Ma

The Great Race
Quang Tri, Vietnam
1967

"No Mac, I'm telling' you. It was Jackie Wilson not Wilson Picket who sang that song." Robby unfolded a can opener from the C-ration box and pulled out a can of ham and lima beans. Lunchtime at our observation post.

I looked over my shoulder at the tree line across the dry rice paddy and returned to our long running debate: Motown.

"You think because I'm white I don't have a memory?"

Robby stared at the last white lima bean inside the can as though it was Frank Sinatra's name on a record label. He looked over at me, sweat glistening on black skin.

"You still don't get it. You're OK, Mac, for a California boy, and lucky enough to have a soul station to listen to while you were safe in your Whitey suburb. But music is a cultural thing Brother, something in the blood, and well, your blood is yours and ours is ours."

We finished eating in silence. We knew the color of blood by then.

"It's time to call in. Check it out. Mac."

I put my can of mixed fruit down and scanned the tree line with binoculars. Nothing. Plastic on the handset was hot so I held it away from my ear and squeezed the button. The rest of the company was dug in for lunch maybe two hundred meters behind us.

"Foxtrot Four. This is OP One. Over.

Static, then Smithy's Southern twang. "Copy. Go."

"Sitrep. All clear. Over."

"Roger. Out." Smitty clicked off.

"Hey Mac, give me that can of mixed fruit and I'll sing the whole song for you and you can admit you're blowing smoke about Wilson Pickett."

"I know the lyrics, Robby, and my voice is better."

"Bullshit! I heard you sing."

"Listen to this." I stood up, took a deep breath and opened my mouth. Nothing came out.

Half way across the rock-hard paddy in front of us, fifty to sixty guerillas were running at full speed. Metal flashed in the sun.

"Holy fuck! Let's go!" I slipped the radio on my back, triggered the phone, and started running.

"Foxtrot Four. OP One. Fifty VC, half a click out moving in. Don't shoot!"

The radio weighed twenty-five pounds and after fifty meters, Robby began to leave me behind. Hot, humid, big dirt clods everywhere and I began to slow down. Robbie stopped. He turned and sank to one knee. The M16 came up and he emptied a clip along side my ear back toward our observation post.

"Come on, Mac!"

He slapped another clip in and that's when we heard it. Chopper blades. Robby pointed north above the tress.

"Fuckin' A! They're makin' a run on us! They think we're VC."

A Cobra gunship on air support lined up on a strafing run four hundred meters out and was coming fast. We all looked the same from the air. Or so I thought, then.

I lay down on my stomach and called in. "Foxtrot. Abort chopper. Friendlies!"

Static.

"Abort! Abort!"

Nothing.

Robby stared at me. I shook my head.

The ship closed to a hundred meters. Robby stood up, unbuckled his helmet and threw it down. He turned his dark face up to the oncoming chopper and an arm went up with the middle finger thrust into the Vietnamese sky.

He screamed. "I'm Black you Muthafucker! Black!"

The Cobra pulled up, swooped over us and turned around to reacquire another target: the front line of the VC troops.

"Forget the radio, Mac!"

We jumped up and waving our arms in the air, sprinted to the outer ring of the company defensive position. No one shot us so we ran inside the circle and dove behind a blasted-out tree stump. Relieved, exhausted, and exhilarated, we laughed while around us Foxtrot opened fire. Hearts pounding together and gasping for air we leaned side by side against the stump.

"I have never been so happy to be so Black in all my Godamned life!"

"Me too Robby, Me too."

He turned to me and smiled with a beauty I'll always remember.

"It *was* Jackie Wilson you know."

"Are there cultures or tribes wherein individuals covet and protect their   cherished memories and never speak of them for fear the retelling might diminish and steal the soul of the experience?"

Mac

NONG SON TRILOGY

I
False Memory?
Reno, NV
1995

"Where the fuck you been for thirty years, Mac?"

A couple oil tanker loads of beer, half a dozen marriages, and complications from combat wounds took its toll on my foxhole buddy. He looked fifteen years older than his fifty-five.

"Tell you the truth, Andy, I've been trying to forget about Vietnam. This is my first reunion. The hotel committee just happened to choose something close to my home."

"Stop feeling so uptight. I know what you did over there, so do these guys, and you got respect from everyone here. I'll get you a drink. Relax."

I looked around the hospitality suite: happy faces, laughter, middle-aged men hugging, hesitant newcomers dragged into small groups and drowned in the deep intimacy shared only by survivors of the same trauma.

A photo display mounted on a sidewall caught my eye and I wandered over to check out the mug book of youthful faces in a far-away land. Standing in the past, skinny young grunts leaned against bunkers and like virgin warriors, posed with weapons and Marlboros.

Red and Chief, Sugar Bear and Smitty, Crazy Eddie and all the others, frozen in time, forever young. Their names? Where did they come from? How many lived, married, had kids, joined the Elks?

Inside a black-and-white snap shot with rippled edges, a young Marine stood on a riverbank smoking a cigarette. A yellow Post-It marked with black pen identified, "Rusty", in front of Nong Son Village."

"Here's a Jack Daniels and water, Mac. You need it."

Andy turned and looked up at Rusty. "He got hit in Hue, didn't make it. Come on. Smitty's over there in his wheel chair and wants to talk to you."

I pointed at Rusty. "I was just thinking about living alone in the village up there. Remember? They sent me in to liaison with the militia and collect Intel under the cover of teaching English. Living with those villagers changed my life. "

Andy stopped smiling. "Yeah. What a fuck job."

"What do you mean? And give me that drink."

Not known for his subtly, the man I trusted with my life many times shook his head. "You dumb fuck, they sent you up there to die."

A swallow of Jack Daniels burned away part of the shock. Why would he come out with something like this? True, he loved his drink and drama, but as a career Marine such a statement implicated his beloved Corps.

"Andy, come over here and sit down and lower your voice."

We found two padded chairs in the corner overlooking Reno below. He flagged down a waiter. "Two more."

Andy leaned back and rubbed his stomach. "The VA put in some kind of material to replace necrotic muscle tissue. The itching drives me crazy."

I waited. He looked up at the photos. "A lot of those guys are dead because of the fuckup on Union II. We all knew it, but you were the only one goin' around talkin' about it, even to the First Sergeant at Battalion. Remember?"

Union II. May 26, 1967. Twelve choppers lifted off with our guys. Three came back. Foxtrot Company used as bait. Foxtrot decimated. Too many body bags. Rows of empty cots. Me and Gunny Green, the only survivors of the CP. Yes, I remembered.

I looked down at the whiskey in my glass. "I can't forget. I tried."

Andy sat up. "The hell you went through that night, I can't imagine. You must have been really messed up for a while 'cause you stared makin' waves. Sayin' shit like, "Cowardice. Leaving our wounded."

They wanted to get rid of you Mac, and not just transfer you, because you would just keep talkin'. I gotta piss. Be right back."

He limped off and I stared at the photos across the room. Dozens dead, betrayed and buried by the god damned Code of Silence. Why had I come to the reunion? The only happy episode from the war, now in jeopardy: Nong Son Village…

Built by French missionaries and miners on the banks of a brown-water river, isolated, beautiful. Eight hundred souls from different levels of Vietnamese society lived in harmony and prosperity. Above them, an eighteen-hundred-foot hill held a company of Marines in three rings of defense. Mortars supplied fire support for ops in the valley.

Along the river stood rows of pastel-colored stucco apartments once occupied by functionaires from the colonial mining operation. One small room with a rope-sling bed and a hole in the floor for a toilet served as my home, office, and "intelligence" gathering center. In the corner on an ammo box, stood my lifeline for rescue, a PRC 25 radio.

As the only American in the ville, I might as well have been on Mars if the shit hit the fan. My qualifications?

56

Two years of English Lit and thee months in an Army language school.

Andy's allegation began to make some kind of strange sense…

II
Teacher, Translator, Soldier, Spy
An Hoa, Vietnam
1967

"Looks like you survived another disaster, Corporal. You gonna run around and make trouble again?"

Fat, pale, and a lifer, our new Ist Sergeant looked up at me from his desk in the safety of the command hooch. Another elementary school dropout from the South. His pressed uniform impressed no one. I could kill him later that night and no one would know. From the looks of the clerks around us, no one would care.

"Lt. Scuras got the word twelve hours before they over ran us, Ist Sergeant."

"Just because you speak Gook, don't mean shit. He did the right thing and his report is now official." After a week in country behind a desk, he seemed to be an expert on combat operations.

Lt. Scuras and I were on delicate terms. A villager, at great personal risk, warned me of VC infiltration before we got over-run on top of Nong Son Hill. Would I inform Battalion? He offered to nominate me for Officer Candidate School. A bribe? A quick transfer? Guilt?

The desk jockey jabbed a folder up at me. "Battalion has an assignment here for you." He grinned and a second chin squeezed out under his first weak one.

I looked around at the typists and admin staff. Only La Barbera from the Old Foxtrot was still around, and he was a short timer. No back up, anywhere.

"Most of the guys from Union II and your fight on top of The Hill are no longer with us. As of today, this includes you. You're gonna go back up there, live in the ville, and liaise with the militia."

Fatso enjoyed power. A punishment in his mind, the transfer was salvation in mine. After seven months, I was an Old Timer and a threat to the new pecking order of non-coms. Foxtrot was full of new replacements due to KIAs, wounded, disease, and rotations back home. Newbies could not be trusted, and they saw those of us leftover from a string of losing battles as bad luck.

And so the day came to load my rifle and briefcase for a new mission: win the hearts and minds of English students, and through them develop trust enough to gather intelligence in a remote village in the midst of a catastrophic civil war.

Two days later, I climbed the metal steps up the side of a colonial coalmine to the abandoned offices and found the designated room. The door stood ajar. The barrel of my rifle nudged it all the way open and poked into the silence.

Behind two folding conference tables sat twenty smiling men varying in age from twenty to eighty years of age, erect, alert. The operational status of the mine continued in limbo, and before me, unemployed professional staff sat in Western clothes next to village elders in loose-fitting traditional pajamas.

Now what?

I nodded and turned away to inventory the classroom. A blackboard with no chalk, an empty bookshelf, and a darkened window etched with coal dust made up the extent of teaching resource materials. Holy shit.

Out side and down the valley, explosions thumped as 80-mm mortar shells walked a trail of support for some poor patrol in trouble. Another day.

My students, all long-time survivors, did not flinch and sat frozen like hungry disciples at The Last Vietnamese Supper. Most of them were older then me. What was I going to do?

I faced the black board and hung my rifle sling on the top corner of the frame. Lt. Scuras had given me his extra map case for lesson plans and materials. So with an empty briefcase I took a breath and turned slowly to face my platoon-strength student body. Shit. I probably shot some of their cousins or brothers.

There in a row, not a single face. Twenty heads of black hair lined up like bowling balls at a bowling alley, bowing in respect, not for me, but for the Teacher!

Seven months of combat did not prepare me for this kind of fear. My legs shook. My brain collapsed. My heart raced. And just as in combat, when all is lost, I invoked the only recourse: prayer.

A voice spoke within me. "Please God, if I ever do anything right, please make it now!"

I addressed the class. "Chao Cac Ong!" (Hello Group Male)

The hairy bowling balls straightened up in sync like a Marine Corps drill team and transformed into twenty smiling Vietnamese men. "Chao Tai!" (Hello Teacher)

And thus began the happiest time of my life and a three-month love affair with a small village, a long time ago

III
Monsoon
Nong Son, Vietnam
1967

"Can you hear me, Mac? Nod your head. Good."

The sound of rain. A waterfall slid off the roof of my hut and poured down over cobblestones running to the Thu Bon River raging below. My fever burned hot and the medic from Echo Company shook his head, his distant voice fighting with the sound of the storm outside. "Mac, I can't get the temperature down. Only thing for that in my kit is aspirin. You gotta drink as much water as you can."

I said nothing. I couldn't.

"We need medivac but a no-fly order is in effect until this storm lets up. I gotta get back up the hill before dark or they might shoot me comin' in. Hate to leave you here alone."

Behind him, four or five of my students stood against a wall.

The security team leader stuck his helmet through the broken window. "Gotta go, Doc. Captain says now."

"See you tomorrow Mac." I felt someone pat my shoulder.

Motion. Whispers. Silence.

Cracks and patches in the ceiling plaster floated and danced above me in beautiful patterns sketching a map of my long journey from Los Angeles to Nong Son.

"We help you, Tai." An elder pulled off my T-shirt and fatigue pants.

Over the river, thunder boomed. Two of the younger men stood me up. "We help, Tai."

I leaned on them as they pulled and hugged me through the front doorway and into the monsoon. And there we stood. Under a torrent of water, two five-foot human crutches supporting a six-foot white ghost.

In just a few minutes, my temperature began to drop. Clarity returned and in a flash of lightening, I saw the smiling faces of my two saviors staring up at me. After fifteen minutes of Vietnamese hydrotherapy, we returned to my room and old Quang dried me off before the three of them laid me back down. He covered me with a dry sheet, tucked me in, and gently wiped my face.

He smiled. "Drink chai. Good." Hot tea stank of rotten roots and dark earth. He folded his arms across his chest and stood like a statue, a midget gunnery sergeant in pajamas.

Quang turned down the lamp, gathered spectators, and left the room. Yet I felt the presence of another, softer energy somewhere nearby. Gradually the ceiling stopped crawling and I began to dream….

…An elderly woman with white hair sat cross-legged at the foot of my bed. In front of her, a charcoal brazier supported and heated a pot of tea. The dancing red glow of coals cast her shadow on the wall as she chanted and rubbed a string of wooden beads back and forth between wrinkled and ancient hands. I slept the sleep of the Dead.

A streak of sunlight splashed across the ceiling. Our monsoon had gone as quickly as it came and taken my fever with it. I felt renewed, born again, lighter in body and spirit. The after-taste of terrible tea from the night before filled my mouth, accompanied by a raging hunger.

Quang leaned against a post in the open doorway, smiling. He nodded in the direction of the far corner and I twisted around to look. The old woman from my dream smiled back as she sliced vegetables, making Pho soup.

Something strange and wonderful was happening to me. The tough combat veteran, now a helpless patient ten thousand miles from home, won over by the hearts and minds of peasants in a remote Vietnamese village.

As a Marine, I was no good after that. The thought of shooting someone, anyone, belonged to a Self who no longer existed. I had been recruited and initiated into the human race. I now knew the real mission: To do as much good for the village in what time I may have left to live.

Something had transformed me from within; charged with purpose and meaning, I was full of energy. My days became fully alive and my body vibrated with urgency and purpose. I didn't want to go to sleep. I knew this new life, this new feeling could end at any moment. I didn't want to miss anything!

As the war around us intensified, I ate and slept in students' homes as they rotated me around like a circuit-riding preacher. Returning to my own room in the mornings, footprints left evidence of midnight visitors. -We never spoke of the danger. And in the Vietnamese way, only a gentle squeeze of my hand while inviting me to dinner sent the darker message that guerillas might visit that same night.

And so began the love affair of my life. Whatever intelligence, creativity, and strength I was born with was called forth, valued, and embraced by those around me. Giving and receiving became one. My naïve suburban soul recognized something very precious and fragile -- filled every moment. It couldn't last......

The war continued around us, and after three months I became a casualty, not of war but of hospitality. Each day students manipulated and competed to bring me home for a meal. While flattered, I knew that my performance as the new oddity in town was much in demand. My repertoire of excruciating tonal accents, a few card tricks, songs, and amusing cultural body language, entertained and distracted families. After many meals of mystery cuisine, I began to lose weight, energy, and the ability to concentrate. River fever ended my stay and Doc of Echo Company called in a medivac.

On the flight to Tripler Hospital in Honolulu, I flirted with a flight attendant while a stream of brown liquid squirted down my leg. I waited to exit the plane last because of brown spots on the seat of my pants. I stared out of the window down as troops waved and yelled to ecstatic relatives waiting behind a temporary chain link fence.

In those days a portable stairway rolled up against the exit door and passengers departed onto the runway. Combat soldiers rushed to happy reunions waiting just a few yards away. Pow! An engine backfired in one of the luggage trucks under our plane.

Half of the disembarking troops dove on the asphalt to take cover and in some sort of schizophrenic, In-between Land hands continued to wave to loved ones while bodies lay face down on the tarmac face. Relatives froze like statues, and for one brief moment, caught a glimpse of the price paid by sons and fathers.

Two months later, soft and civilian, the hospital released me and I returned to Foxtrot in Phu Bai, Vietnam. With three weeks left on my tour of duty, I drew new gear as Fox saddled up for Hue City and the Tet New Year Offensive. Much has been written, filmed, and documented of that battle that I prefer to bury it in the shadows. In the midst of the Offensive, my tour expired.

I joined a few others on a truck back to Phu Bai and on to Da Nang for a flight to EL Toro Marine Corps Air Station, in California. Three days after landing, I exited through the front gates as a civilian with seven hundred bucks and no plan.

PART THREE

So I returned to my home port, lost and adrift. I knew that while civilians around me embraced the same world I had left, there was no place in it for me. The consciousness, aspirations, and dreams of my childhood no longer meant anything.

I lingered. My high school sweetheart had planned our marriage, and for a month, I pretended to have returned from war - unchanged. Full of anxiety and guilt, I packed a bag and my roommate dropped me off at the local airport. What to do? After a few beers, I looked up at the departure board and bought a ticket to Hawaii.

Construction jobs ended in brawling and drinking with work crews. An older neighbor saw my future and arranged an interview with an agency looking for a counselor with emotionally disturbed boys. My knowledge of the subject was thorough.

A new work-week began and I dropped into a volcano of hormones, hysteria, and hyper-activity. A dozen boys, more damaged than I, needed boundaries, love, constancy, and a role model. I forgot about my own wounded psyche, focused on this wild pubescent gang: my new family. As the boys came to accept me, my own healing began.

Working at the Salvation Army Home for Boys shaped a civilian identity and launched a career of advocacy for the disenfranchised and under-privileged. Not much had changed: I again had a mission and this time with a new enemy: bureaucracy

Everything went well in Honolulu until the director offered me a promotion in recognition of the bond which had developed with the boys. Habits die hard, and as in combat, I avoided being singled out in a group, for therein lay danger. I fled.

"Now, you will not swell the rout
Of lads who wore their welcome out,
Runners whom renown outran
And the name died before the man."
To an Athlete Dying Young
A.E. Houseman

Full Circle
Bellaire, TX
1969

"Come on, Mac. Put your shit in your bag and we'll drive you over there. His family knows you're coming and they're waiting."

Even though shot in the ass last year, Ron still played Boy Scout with what passed for *joie de vivre* in Texas. Jimmie smiled his big country-boy smile content, with his traditional role as Sidekick. They scouted the hotel room for my clothing and personal items. Soon a small pile grew on the top of the bed.

"Grab his bag, Jimmie. It's in the closet."

I still wasn't ready after a long train ride across the South West. I needed time; time to figure out what I was going to say to Mike's folks. Instead of going directly to their home, I had rented a room downtown and called some Marine Corps pals in Houston.

While I was a decorated Marine, multilingual world traveler, and held a PhD in charming bullshit, I was terrified. Somewhere between fulfilling a promise to the parents of a deceased friend and my talent for high drama, I was about to navigate new territory without a compass or map.

"OK, Ron. I'll go, but I need a drink." Both Texans smiled.

The three of us had studied and drank our way through the Defense Language Institute in Monterey, California. We stumbled through the Vietnamese program and somehow wound up together in the same battalion in 'Nam.

Now here we were a year after our tours, in our prime, full of hormones in Houston, Texas, and heading for the hotel bar. Eleven thousand miles from Vietnam and in civilian clothes, we entered the elevator on yet another patrol.

By midnight, liquid courage flowed through me and I recited a poem by Ferlinghetti pissing, of every Catholic in hearing distance. Something about, "Jesus, Being all hung up...."

Ron heard it all before. "OK, Mac. Enough. Jimmie and I have to work tomorrow. Your bag is in the car. Let's go."

In the back seat, I watched skyscrapers dissolve into suburbia as we turned from the boulevard onto a residential street. Ron stopped his Valiant and turned the engine off. "Here it is. The lights are still on so just go on up and knock on the door."

I leaned forward between the two of them. "Aren't you coming in with me?"

Jimmie shook his head. "Damn it, Mac. They ain't the Viet Cong you know. Now go do it."

As I walked up the path to the house, Ron and Jimmie watched to make sure I did my duty and that someone answered the doorbell.

I dropped my bag on the porch, stared at a little white button, and after a minute, pushed it. Four notes belled softly inside, chairs scraped, voices, footsteps. The doorknob turned. My heart drummed loudly and I stood like a frozen statue under the porch light. The door swung open.

"Mac!"

And there they were. Mike's parents. Just as I imagined. They hugged, kissed, and dragged me inside. My anxiety dissolved in a frontal assault of love and celebration. I turned around to see Ron and Jimmie nodding and smiling. The Valiant pulled away from the curb. Mission accomplished.

A year of correspondence with Mike's mother sketched a family portrait of wholesome Americana devastated by the loss of their beloved son. Now, a little overdue perhaps, a friend had traveled to their home to help replace a two year old, yellowing telegram.

In the following week I lived an entire lifetime. Mike's dad and I stayed up nights until neighborhood dogs barked at the paperboy in the morning. As a survivor of the

Battle of the Bulge in WWII, we found common ground and language.

Loquacious, capable, and dynamic, Mrs. Driscoll played tour guide as we attended church, visited Mike's high school, turned the pages of family albums, and then, one day, stood before her son' grave.

"Do you like his epitaph, Mac?"

I read the carving on the tombstone. 'Corporal Victor Michael Driscoll, 1945-1967, USMC, Vietnam.'

"Yes. It's fine."

But Mike was not a typical Marine. Sensitive, articulate, and kind, he seemed miscast in the violence of combat. He carried an aura of fatalism, and those of us with many months of experience sensed that he would not survive.

I slept in his old room and was encouraged to make it my own. Inside an old wooden trunk, I found a huge stack of notebooks filled with poetry written by Mike, and I read it all. Romantic, idealistic, he wrote on the theme of dying bravely and young: Then I understood: a self-fulfilling prophecy. Perhaps he got what he wanted.

Ron fixed me up with a great gal, Jimmie gave me his old car, a friend of Mr. Driscoll offered me a job, and my friendship with Mike's fourteen-year-old brother flourished and deepened. Bellaire, Texas gave the homecoming I never received in my own community. Everything was great. It was all so wonderful - and terrifying.

I began to feel I might become a replacement for Mike. It was time to go.

The Driscolls understood. They hugged me and agreed that everything had happened too fast and I needed to leave and "find myself". As she poured more coffee, Mrs. Driscoll smiled at her son's athletic awards mounted on the family-room wall.

The back door popped open and Mike's brother tossed his baseball mitt on top of the TV. "What's up?"

Mrs. Driscoll held my gaze and nodded.

What could I possibly say? "How was practice? Let's go talk in the bedroom."

For a week he was happy to talk of grown up stuff and share secrets his parents might have found uncomfortable. He had lost his big brother, and now I was about to leave.

In Mike's room we stood in front of the window and stared out at the backyard where two brothers wrestled, played catch, told secrets, and planned their futures.

I looked down at him and confessed, "It's time for me to leave here. I thought I was coming to help you guys and I'm the one who got all the good stuff."

He looked back again outside at the rusty swing set. "You are my brother now."

Oh shit. The last thing I wanted to happen. Would he follow Mike and I, enlist and come home lost and confused, or not at all?

I struggled. He felt my hesitation.

His hand felt warm on my arm and like an older brother he looked at me and said, "It's OK, Mac. I love you." His hand fell away. "But I don't wanna be like you."

That night, the Greyhound Bus agent sold me a ticket for Bloomington, Indiana. L.T. Brown from our infantry training regiment said he had a bedroom for rent and a job at the pizza parlor in town.

Soon

The soon to die
Parade in review,
Replacements for
The already dead.
We, the almost dead
Many times,
Search for the mark
Of the Beast

Among these
Clean-clothed
Baby-faced,
Well fed
Bodies

Assembled
In formation,
Their fate
Already written
In ancient script...

Known only by us:
The almost dead.
The plot, a mystery,
The timing, soon.
Death's name signed
On a contract
Made long ago.

These Chosen
Stand with one boot
In the grave.
And through grace,
Are blind.

Yet
We are mute.
To call out, to interfere-
The Beast may turn
His gaze...
Our way.

Our own time
will come.
Our contract
With this dark shadow
Is already

Signed,
Mac

"Wandering through many countries and over many seas,
I come, my brother, to these many obsequies......
To speak in vain to your silent ashes."
Gaius Catullus
57 B.C.

INTELLIGENCE TRILOGY

I

No Escape
Bamako, Mali, Africa
1974

He looked about thirty years older than me and a bit lonely. So I did my part and sat down next to him. "What's your program?

"Citrus tree propagation. You?"

"Water wells. Just got here."

"I leave soon for Niger River Valley region. How about a cup of coffee?"

"Not that instant crap please. The stuff gives me heart burn."

"I grew up in the Depression. Come on up for some real coffee, Cowboy coffee."

"Sounds good."

Our dormitory held a variety of Peace Corps Volunteers studying language and culture. My new friend from the Southern California orange groves lived on the top floor with a nice breeze. A hotplate soon glowed red and he sprinkled grounds on top of water boiling in one of the local aluminum pots. Smelled good.

"This your wife?" A couple of framed pictures stood side by side on top of the dresser.

"Yes, she passed away a few years ago." Only the sound of water bubbling and boiling.

"I'm sorry. This must be your son here? Looks like a Marine boot camp photo."

He came over, stood next to me. Silence.

I picked up the photo. "Good looking. Where's he stationed?"

"He was killed in Vietnam."

"Oh."

Shit. Six years after Nam and ten thousand miles deep into the Southern Sahara. Where did I have to go to get away? My neighbor was hurtin,' so as a former Marine, I did my part.

"What happened?"

"All I know is, he was killed in the fall of 1967 on an operation called Hastings. No information, just a telegram.

But I knew. I knew exactly what happened. And again, I had done my part...

II
The Long Yesterday
Nong Son Village
1967

"Have some hot tea, Mr. Mac." He was much older than I and overweight, unusual for rural Vietnamese, even for a militia officer.

"Thank you Captain Thuy."

Nong Son's Catholic Church now held military and provincial administrative offices. Old Father Nguyen had fled to the safety of Da Nang long ago. The religion of French colonials no longer aligned commoners with powers struggling for control in their latest war. To enter and pray at Mass in an outlying region pinned a bull's eye on the back of any Catholic survivor from another time, another foreign occupier.

"How is your family, Captain Thuy? A new picture of your son perhaps?"

He smiled the smile of all proud fathers. "Yes. Here in drawer." The small black- and-white photo held a serious boy in a provincial school uniform.

"Thank you for bring Doctor Viti and help my wife."

In his culture, he was now indebted. I nodded and slurped some tea.

We spoke of family, food, and boredom. All the safe stuff. I waited and at the right moment, put my half-full cup on his desk. He nodded and poured more tea: a signal that staff had left for lunch in the village.

He looked over at the closed door then pushed a map of the local valley across his desk.

"They dig graves."

"Where?"

His chubby finger landed on a ville half way to An Hoa. "Here."

"How do you know?" Graves meant the enemy would stand and fight long enough to bury their dead. Very rare.

"My uncle have farm. They make him dig in trees. They come at night. Bring supplies."

Jesus. Two months of living alone in the ville and my first bit of intelligence. Had I won at least one heart and mind? If so, Thuy was taking a huge risk.

"Your name will not be spoken. Marines will send their own scouts to verify."

"Thank you, Mr. Mac. Now we must eat." A towel came off the tray on the corner of the desk, a feast from my favorite cook, his wife.

An hour later, I caught a ride up the hill to the command bunker of the Marine security company. The Captain listened to my story and turned to his battalion radioman in the corner.

"Call An Hoa and get me the Colonel. Good work, Mac. Maybe this will turn out to be something."

Village life flowed along and some pen-pal letters arrived from my old high school for my English students. As we read aloud in class, the soft "thump, thump" of heavy mortars traveled across the valley. Aircraft raced down the river at low altitude. Another operation launched.

Three days later, I ran into Andy as he got off the metal ferryboat on a resupply run from An Hoa.

"Hey Mac. How's the easy life?"

"Good. What's the news from Battalion?"

He dropped his pack on the riverbank and lit a cigarette. "Major fuck up as usual. Couple of days ago they sent out eight birds full of Echo Company on some op called Hastings. Seems they got info that the gooks were gonna stand and fight."

I got that bad feelin in my gut. "What happened?

"No recon. No prep, nothin. Scuttle butt says they flew right to the coordinates. Guys got shot as they jumped off the choppers. The gooks were there all right. Mortars came in. Too late."

He tossed his cigarette in to the river and watched it float down stream. "What's the matter, Mac?"

I couldn't speak. I felt hollow, empty of all hope for redemption. Never again would I pass information to anyone.

It was all insanity, meaningless.

III
Back in Bamako
Mali, Africa
1974

I gently replaced the young Marine's photo on the dresser. Had I killed him? Did Thuy give me Intel to set up an ambush? I should have known command would fuck it up.

Time and ten thousand miles... no escape...

"It is a good thing to escape from death,
But it is not great pleasure
To bring death to a friend."
Sophocles, 495-406 B.C.

How Shakespeare Saved My Life
Sonoma State University, CA
1974

"Today we'll finish the last scene in Julius Caesar. Over the weekend read Hamlet' and we will begin discussion on thematic parallels within the two plays during Tuesday's class."

About a dozen of us sat in a circle, a circle designed to lubricate intimacy and to create an audience for those of us assigned to read aloud. It was a summer class, the last one available and I had signed up to qualify for a stipend offered by the GI Bill. It seemed Shakespeare was not highly regarded by administration, for our classroom had no windows. It was hot, just like the battlefield scene we were about to review.

I was older than the others by a dozen years, enrolled in my fifth university, postponing any effort to re-enter mainstream America and beginning not to care. Like other citadels of learning, we had a base with many buildings, instructors to train us, specialty schools, comrades, and graduation for successful study. Of course, we were all just warm bodies replacing the casualties, dropouts, graduates, and no-shows. Without student fodder there would be no tenure for career lifers. Shakespeare helped pay the rent for both the professor and me.

Dorothy Overly was a tough broad, around fifty-five, kinda ugly and wide. Yet our professor was full of energy and dramatic expression. She reminded me of the middle-aged buck sergeant from Alabama who taught a heavy weapons class at Camp Pendleton. We would gratefully remember the lessons he forced into us.

Overly turned slowly inside our circle, capturing each of us in turn, daring us not to care.

"Understanding what the classics have to offer is truly a gift from antiquity, a past with characters who have confronted the slings and arrows of life's misfortune. We here must all face many of the same misfortunes in the course of living out our own life's script. Some of us already have."

Why was she looking at me?

She took a step closer. "Actually feeling their exquisitely chronicled lives is a blessing that connects us to humankind and to our own soul. Observing and applying these universal lessons can more fully integrate our own personal past and help us to face the yet unknown challenges to come. But this, my fellow travelers, requires feeling."

She took her seat between two students with complexion challenges and opened her purse. Pulling out a tissue box, she set it in front of her on the desk. A pack of Camels peeked out from the still-open handbag.

"Check today's guideline and find the part assigned to you. Let us take ten minutes and silently read scene 5. Rumor has it that we all have hearts and souls. Some of you may even have experience. Use these. Try to match your emotions to the character's situation, and imagine being him, being there, long ago."

Then sitting in her chair, staring at nothing, Dorothy Overly went away. Not day- dreaming, really gone. I had seen it in combat many times. Maybe she was a Buddhist or something or just burned out on students taking her classes to accumulate credits. Or maybe she had at one time left her books, her dead authors, and lived a life Shakespeare might have written.

Scanning the assignment, I found my new identity: Brutus, a good guy but he got drafted and joined the wrong cause. Our similarity ended there. He had his own legion. I had a rifle and a pack. Up to now, Julius Caesar had accurately portrayed the classical functions of all politicians and officer corps: ambition.

So I picked up my book and flipped through to the last act. Opposing generals were whining and arguing about who fragged Caesar and why. Meanwhile, honest legionnaires whose names were never recorded waited on the field to die. Shakespeare sure got that part right. Maybe he served in the military. I kept reading.

The battle began. It was all very familiar stuff: poor Intel, lousy communications, tactical blunders, the usual chaos. My guy Brutus moved too fast and the shit started rolling down hill. His side lost and nobody wanted to be taken prisoner. Just like in Nam. About to be overrun, one of the generals, Cassius, committed suicide. Good thing he did it right. The Romans did not have guns and after using a knife or sword on themselves, half the time they woke up in a tent with the enemy smiling down at them. Not good. I kept reading.

Act Five. Scene Five. Julius Caesar

The armies of Mark Anthony and Octavius have defeated the legions commanded by the conspirators who assassinated Caesar. Capture is worse than death.

Brutus to Strato:
Thou art a fellow of good respect
Thy life hath some smatch of honor in it.
Hold then my sword, and turn away thy face
While I do run upon it. Wilt thou Strato?
Strato:
Give me your hand first. Fare you well my lord.
Brutus:
0
Farewell, good Strato. Caesar, now be still.

I killed not thee with half so good a will.
Dies.

A solider helping his friend to die? A mutual obligation? An act of love? I started feeling funny, kinda frozen-like. In those days, I couldn't sleep, and sometimes I got a little disjointed, but this was just a class in a suburban school, just a book.

Tropical perfume from the student next to me floated over my desk, her pungent plumeria blending with my nervous sweat. I looked around and the circle of desks faded into fog from the Central Highlands. Underneath me, brown linoleum tile transformed into rice paddy dirt. And scattered like rag dolls, a ring of bodies rose up out of the past.

I heard Okie's voice. But this time, I was awake.

Final Scene. Operation Union II

Foxtrot Company is about to be overrun by superior forces of the North Vietnamese Army. Okie has been gut shot.

Okie to Mac:

Do it, Mac! Please! You stay, you die!

Mac:

Jesus Okie. Jesus!

Okie:

I'm dead any way. Don't let em get me!

The enemy approaches, torturing, executing
wounded on the field.
Mac to Okie crying:
Goodbye Okie.
Okie:
Thank you.
Mac kills Okie and flees.

"Wake up Mr. MacKinnon. Page 82, line 23 if you please." She was staring at me from across the circle, across time. Somehow I got through the reading and back home to the trailer court. And then the strangest thing of all happened: I slept through the night for the first time in years.

At the end of the semester our professor hosted a class party at her town house a few miles from the university, a civilized affair. Well-read undergrads tried to impress each other and our much-loved mentor. Later in the evening, my hostess and I found ourselves alone at the snack table.

She smiled her big-tooth smile and sipped from a tumbler of Irish whiskey. A gold band suggested a husband, but there was no other evidence in the living area or adjoining rooms.

She gave me The Look. "Are you Mac or Brent?"

I kept chewing the miniature quiche knowing this was a moment not to hide behind a camouflage of humor. "I don't know, Dorothy."

"Come with me." She took my hand and we wove our way through the conversations, flirtations, and wannabe intellectuals. We closed the den door behind us and she crossed over to the desk and opened the top drawer. An old black and white photo in a tarnished silver frame floated on a sea of letters written in a masculine hand.

She drained her glass and smiled. "Meet my husband."

Dorothy Overly put an arm around my waist. A Marine in combat fatigues and parka sitting on snow covered sandbags smiled up at us from the desk. You could tell, he was one of the rare ones thriving in the most difficult of circumstances, his spirit soaring, senses electric, at home with his comrades.

"This is my Charlie. He was killed at the Chosin Reservoir twenty-five years ago."

She became very still and I knew then the place she visited in these moments. I looked up. Marine memorabilia on the opposite wall began to blur and I felt the presence of bare Korean hills in winter, the rainforest of Vietnam, and the dusty plains outside of Rome.

"He was always just Charlie, wherever he was. That's the secret, my friend."

She sighed, straightened up, and put Charlie back in that special place where she kept him.

"Come on. I need a drink. And, Mac?"

"Yes, Dorothy?"

"Will Shakespeare was there with you."

Gook Lover

Graduate School
Fredonia, New York
1981

The day arrived when faculty advisors asked me to choose a topic for my Master's thesis in the Linguistic Department. What to do? Maybe some coffee and pie at the local restaurant would lubricate my imagination.

Sitting at the counter, I stared across at fat round pies under glass. Indecision seemed to be the flavor of the day and I couldn't decide between apple and rhubarb, cold or hot, alamode or not.

The white jacket of a bus boy stopped in front of me holding a glass of water. "Wata?"

And there, holding a tray of water glasses stood my thesis: a Vietnamese refugee.

Over the next month, Vinh Lu came to my apartment three nights a week after work on his way home to Dunkirk. He was thrilled that an American on the distant planet of Upstate New York once visited his own land, spoke his language and both of us, survivors of the war.

I tape recorded interviews, made notes for my thesis, and when trust found its way into our hearts, asked Vinh to tell me of his life in Vietnam. He had just been relocated to the US from a refugee camp in the Philippines, and true to Vietnamese character, he poured out his memories in a flood of emotion.

During our last week together he brought his diary to my home and with the help of his English, my Vietnamese, and a bilingual dictionary, we struggled, and translated excerpts at random.

The Diary of Vinh Lu
Quang Tri Provence
Vietnam

From the Diary
Song Vau Village
February 12, 1980

They are all dead now, all except me.

My brother Binh died yesterday here in our village holding a rake out in front of him like the rifle he once carried so well. His last target was the resident ghost of an enemy who over the years had become his friend. Nights around the fire, Binh laughed and told us the dead American boy waited for him in the next life. They are together now; gone to that place we all must one-day visit.

The war had made Binh unafraid. In those rare moments when he did not smile, he stared into the darkness over the river and provoked the shadow world with his whispers, "We shall meet soon."

Only in this did he move from the common heart we all shared in our village. And while we feared the many phantoms around us, we forgave Binh a thousand times, for he was ever our friend, our living spirit, and the best among us. We loved him like no other.

Our land is full of ghosts, wandering souls who died violently, ripped from their bodies and their unfinished lives. Confused and with no living family to honor them, no altar where they receive veneration and nourishment, they cannot guide new generations through this troubled land. Their fate is to wander, wander without purpose, without end.

A poet to the last, Binh fell face down in this season's harvest, his thin body pushing up a gentle fog of rice dust. Pierced and illuminated by the morning sun, the mist wrapped him in a shining shroud. I watched his last breath flow silently out his scarred body without complaint and become one with the mist. In tender caress, pollen settled upon him, blessing his last moment.

This small cloud was his only cremation. We no longer had wood to coffin our dead. Profiteers stripped our valley of hardwood a decade after the War of Liberation against the Americans. Our young people care nothing for the past know almost nothing of history, and the always-corrupt Southerners exploit our future as they ape the lifestyle of the foreigners who almost destroyed us. What did we really win? The poor remain poor. It seems only the face of the tax collector changes.

Binh and I once felt the excitement of youth. Are all young men so easily seduced by promises of a glorious cause? Did the American boy who Binh killed believe the propaganda in his own village? I remember when the political officer first came to us and began the classes, our first of many. Most of all I remember his announcement that soon the men of my village must volunteer.

Diary Excerpt
Son Vau Village
April 9, 1963

All the men of our village sat on the ground in obedient rows, legs crossed with calloused, anxious hands folded in our laps. Why were we not in the fields? Facing us, six armed guerrillas stood side by side, and in front of them, a small tidy man in a Northern uniform.

He did not smile. "After a hundred years our victorious national forces expelled the French, their imperialist occupation, and their hired mercenaries, The Legion.

"Peace and reunification of our country seemed near. Our hearts were joyful and full of gratitude, but in a last dishonorable act, the French armed and anointed their Catholic puppets. Branding our beloved national leader and our People's Army, "Communist," they looted the last of our treasury and sailed away.

He nodded towards the border. "True, we now accept help from the Northern Dragon. When no one else steps forward, then a bargain must be struck. The cost of business with Beijing is always high. We will deal with them in the season of reckoning. Now in their fear, the Southerners welcome yet another devil from the West."

Binh could talk without moving his lips, and just as in our lower form school days, his goal was to cause me to laugh so that I might reap a rich harvest of consequence. It was a game we played. I owe him much for this gift. He forced me to think and speak quickly, early training for my later career.

His whisper mimicked the nasal pinch of the northern official.

"And as soon as Comrade Dwarf removes the sugar cane stalk from up his ass, we can plant it and see what the harvest will really be."

I managed to choke down a giggle with a spasm of gagging. Binh pounded me on my back and apologized to our guest.

"A childhood affliction, Comrade. He may not be fit for a Home Defense Team."

Healed instantly by the political officer's silence, I sat at attention, put on my respectful face, and waited.

"Your name, Afflicted One?"

"Vinh Lu, sir."

"Our first team assignment will assist you in regaining your health and through this, perhaps appropriate behavior. You will assume command of daily drills on the soccer field. Consider this an opportunity."

"Yes Comrade."

"May I assume that your partner in this little charade is your twin?"

"Yes Comrade."

"His privilege is to write daily evaluations of your performance as drill instructor."

Binh smiled and saluted. "Yes Comrade!"

Our instructor turned his narrow shoulders to us and pointed to a map of Quang Tri Province nailed on a tree. Few of us had ever visited the locations drawn on the map. Why would we? Our land, our animals and the Thu Bon River sustained, nurtured, and healed us. All this was soon to change.

I squirmed and mumbled. "What's a drill?"

Diary
February 12, 1980
Son Vau Village

Binh is gone now. Across from me, his chair sits empty and the chessboard calls out, aching to come alive like a rice paddy in dry season. Our game waits for troops to move back and forth, striking now from a distance, now close enough to touch the enemy and always manipulated by hands from above.

Sometimes when the wind blows down from the mountain, I can still hear our voices as we played at war....

Diary
February 1, 1980
Son Vau Village

I opened with King's pawn and asked my opponent, "Do you think the Americans honor their ancestors as we do?"

Binh sat across from me, our chessboard serving as venue for yet another discussion.

"Their dead tell us stories."

He stared at his hands and at their twin shadows cast down upon red earth behind my house. The hand with the missing two fingers dug into his vest pocket.

"Why do I still carry this?" He slid a faded photograph across the chessboard.

The past rushed over our soldiers on the board and pulled us back into the time of suffering. In the picture, an old couple stands on a porch somewhere in America. They are waving at their loved one as they have for seventeen years and always will -until the photo finally fades and like their beloved family member, they too disappear.

Binh rubbed the stumps above his knuckles and moved his knight forward into jeopardy.

"He took my fingers and I took his life. Why does my hand itch only when I think of him?"

"Binh, you itch for you know the young peasants they sent here to fight were like us, pawns in the hands of greater players in a game we could not imagine. They died as we died, calling out to mothers or sweethearts and clutching photos not of leaders but of family." Camouflaged by two pawns my bishop slid into position.

"Perhaps you are right, Vinh. I still see him in my dreams. A child, really."

He looked down at the board, saw the danger, and asked quietly, "Where is your picture?"

Under my bed inside a cracked and peeling plastic card, a strange Western man wore grey robes. In one hand, he held a long tree branch, curved and pointing down. His other hand held a cross. I was frightened by his beard, and I seldom pulled him out from his hiding place. At first, blood covered the plastic but over the years it dried and flaked away. A thumbprint in blood once pressed upon the chest of the man, but it too gradually faded.

Binh asked, "Do you ever think of the boy whose fingers held that image? Could it be his father? A farmer perhaps, with many buffalo?"

I thought for a moment and answered. "During my only trip to the South, I passed a Catholic church. A man sat behind a folding table, selling pieces of paper. Thinking they were lottery tickets, I opened my purse to buy one."

"And one for me of course!" smiled Binh.

"Of course, Honored Brother. As I handed him one hundred dong, I saw that the paper held not numbers, but pictures, pictures of Western men and women in ancient costumes like our puppets wear in historical dramas. Among these many images lay the bearded man!

"The peddler seller saw my curiosity and said, 'Friend, I see you are on a journey from the country, and as a Catholic your eyes are drawn to our holy Saint Christopher. He will protect you until you return home.'"

Binh asked, "Did the American soldier come from a famous family of priests, or do his people buy an image and pray for protection?"

I took his knight and added it to my pile. "Obviously the spirit in the picture did not do his job."

My brother studied his shrinking number of troops. "He would have been better off with a lottery ticket, perhaps."

"Yes, these were a strange people" I said. " They sent their sons far away to die or go mad. Who will take care of their parents when they are old? Their family line is broken. There will be no new generation to honor their lives, no wisdom for new generations, and no memory of their passing."

Triggering an ambush, Binh placed my queen in jeopardy. "Why did they come?"

"These things I studied when I interrogated prisoners. They brought with them strange words, words the French did not bring. There is no translation and thus, no understanding. Here, I wrote them in my memory book. "Democracy. Communism." Some kind of city government officials perhaps. I do not know."

We stared at the chess pieces on the same board we used as boys, the same pieces when Binh had all his fingers and my wife and child still lived.

Binh sighed. "Well, at least we have peace now."

Around us, our longtime neighbors: poverty and illness, did not disagree.

Diary
April 12, 1964
Son Vau Village

"Go get some oranges for Grandmother." Binh laughed and entered the front yard of his fiancé and her parents.

Grandmother's spirit voice echoed in my ear. "Buy the small plump ones. You know I love those!"

I turned onto the market road and away from the soccer field and my friends. My grandparents live with us at home but only in black-and-white photos fading slowly away, just as they did in life.

My Apartment
Fredonia, New York, 1981
Vinh Lu, Interview Notes

Vinh stared out of my window at the falling snow. "One day, the images on photos will disappear completely. But not until another generation becomes one with their stories, accomplishments, and most importantly, their names. No one dies there. Each day their names are on the lips and in the hearts of family and friends. Not to be remembered, not to continue contributing to future generations; to suffer such a fate would be as though one had never existed

"Our people pray, not to a statue or image of a God, nor do we practice ancestor worship as the French assumed. No invisible god such as the Catholic missionaries brought with them can contribute as our ancestors have, as the land does, and as we will to our own decedents.

"These photographs conjure more than nostalgia. The wisdom they passed on to us emanates from these photos; their faces speak to us of the teaching and hold the center of our moral compass.

"We honor them daily with their favorite fruits, flowers, incense, and a candle to symbolize the goodness they bring. The flow of generations moves through us, joined forever to the past and to the future of our own children. One day I will smile down upon my children from the wall in our American home and worry them with right thought and right behavior!

"Any family member who is blessed to live beyond a half century is revered as the repository of our collective life and is sought out for guidance in matters both public and private. We harvest these sweet fruits from the sages and cook a recipe for our own palate, satisfying our hunger for the divine in everyday life.

"My grandparents and their parents survived the Chinese Mandarins, the French, the Japanese, and the French again. These barbarians came uninvited to our land. All left, defeated by the ancient wisdom, stubbornness, and sacrifice of our ancestors.

"In our village few of us knew how to read, but this changed. The only gift of the French and their imperialist missionaries is their alphabet. We now use their system to read and write Vietnamese, replacing many complicated Chinese characters.

"During the occupation, the French collected men from our region and forced them to labor for their plantations, forestry, and railroad construction. Disguised as a penalty for the failure to pay taxes, many conscripts never returned, or limped home as amputees, punishment for lack of cooperation during servitude.

"After a century, those hard days faded away along with the French but as it has always been our fate, peace came to visit and stayed but a brief season.

"Then you came, Mr. Mac."

Diary
April 12, 1964
Son Vau Village

The oranges smelled delicious, full of the sweet goodness of our land and ripened by the waters of the Thu Bon. I was tempted. But as a child my knuckles were often red, rapped by my mother's weaving stick each time I reached for ripe offerings on the alter.

"Ah, here you are at last!" Grandma smiled at me from inside her picture on the alter.

Diary
April 20, 1966
Son Vau

Each evening, round our village fire pit we shared concerns. We saw no enemy, yet voices in river villages spoke of news from An Hoa to the east. Whispers of large machines tearing the skin off our land, destroying homes to make a place for airplanes. Where would the people live? How would they live? What of dignity? Stripped of ancestral fields and food, they must join other refugees, wandering.

A scraping sound in the dark announced the arrival of Trang. Leaning on his cane, he dragged his foot behind him and lowered his twisted body on the log next to me. Both honored and shunned each day, Trang was a constant reminder of the torture and abuse of foreign occupation.

He laid his cane across his lap and, as always, we listened. "This thing we must not do!"

Trang stared at each one of us sitting around the counsel fire. Such direct expression in public is permitted only by elders.

He stirred the fire with a stick and pointed at our graveyard in the sacred plot. Smoke rose up from the end of the smoldering twig, drifted up through the trees, and dissolved.

"My great uncle cleared that land. I do not approve of digging up his bones so Northerners can tunnel and hide underground like assassins."

Stick in hand. Trang signed his death warrant. Informers were already among us. The harmony we had known in Son Vau was no more.

No one spoke. Trang spit his red beetle nut chew on the ground, rose, turned his back on us, and hobbled into the darkness.

Diary
May 1, 1966
Son Vau

Midday. Six of us stood in near darkness around his sleeping platform in the back of the hut. He lay motionless staring at patterns of thatch in the ceiling.

Binh tried his best. "You have your family, Trang, and all of us will help."

"I cannot provide for my family. I am no longer a man. They should have taken my life. Not this!"

An arm rose up. Cloth used for filtering our drinking water covered his stump while leather straps wound tightly around his right wrist.

"My work now? I am half man and half ghost who walks our village, a symbol of their Northern power, a half-dead spirit to put fear into your hearts.

"You offer your help, and my heart is full of gratitude." He looked away. "And full of shame. I am old and have seen much. This I say and then will say no more for my life is finished: They came for my hand and soon they will come for you."

Binh touched my elbow. We thanked Trang for his wisdom and walked home without speaking. Smoke from charcoal cooking fires drifted up and melted together, forming a grey cloud that gradually floated down over the river.

Mother stood waiting on the stone threshold of the front door.

"Did you bring the onions?"

Our hands held nothing. Trang filled our thoughts. I pointed at Binh, but too late. His finger was already up in position aiming at me.

"One of you get the bottle of nuoc mam from the creek and the other go find your story-telling father. I will use the sweet onions I was saving for your wedding, Vinh."

We turned in opposite directions and left on our assignments. Without looking, I knew Mother stood in the doorway arms folded over her heart's eye, watching her twin sons run off to play, as she had for two decades.

My Apartment
Fredonia, NY, 1981

Vinh pulled a tattered photograph from his shirt pocket. Outside, snow continued to fall.

"This is Mother." He slid her back into the pocket over his heart. "She died on boat. "

He stood and tried to smile. "One day I will smile down upon my children from the wall in our American home and worry them with right thought and right behavior!"

O'Doul's Pub
Fredonia, NY, 1981

My thesis found approval and I graduated that same semester. To this day I reflect on the long reach of the God of War and wonder if any of us who survived, will ever be free of His touch.

"Afghanistan: the place where empires go to die."
Anonymous

Common Ground
Soviet Union
1985

The letter arrived late one September morning just after he turned eighteen. There was nothing special about it, just another business-sized envelope with his name.

Yet letters came rarely for Peter. Then he noticed the envelope had no stamp. It didn't need one; the government didn't use stamps. Looking down at his name, Peter understood that his life had just changed - perhaps forever.

"Other guys in my class had received notices to appear for a physical exam, but the Army wasn't taking everybody then, and I thought somehow they might overlook me."

But Peter wasn't overlooked. He reported for military training and along with others from his hometown was assigned to a transport unit as a tank driver. His battalion shipped out to the war, and seven months later, Peter and his tank drove over a land mine in Afghanistan. With fragments of shrapnel still in his back, he returned home to discover that not only the war but that he, too, was unpopular.

With little or no help from family, community, or government he began to drink heavily and use drugs. Only much later did he find other veterans and join their group. Recovery began, and he slowly regained hope and direction.

Another American boy and Vietnam vet, drafted, damaged, and deranged? No. Peter Tamarov was wounded in Jalalabad, Afghanistan, while serving with the Soviet Army in 1987.

Like our Vietnam, Iraq, and Afghanistan troops, the "Afgansty" were sent to fight in a foreign country, against an invisible enemy, and in a war that made no sense. After combat trauma, survivors returned to an indifferent society and faced their challenges of readjustment with little or no support.

Mac's Diary
Moscow, 1988

(On November 6, 1988, a group of twenty-nine Americans gathered in Copenhagen and after a briefing flew on to Moscow. This coalition of veterans, psychologists, lawyers, specialists in artificial limbs, and organizers formed a delegation to meet one-on-one with Soviet counterparts. Dr. Sandy Scull and I, from Northern California, joined the group.)

A cold wind roared as the bus pulled to a stop at the park where the Afgansy war memorial had been built. Making our way through a foot of snow, a vision of The Vietnam Wall flashed in our common mind. Here we faced a simple granite stone, perhaps six feet tall with a bronze plaque in the middle.

Negotiating for permission to build this testimonial to The Hidden War took years. Even now, local veteran groups are in competition for implementing future expansion of their memorial. As Soviet troops rotate home from Afghanistan, established clubs in home towns wait to welcome them and ease their re-entry. The distrust and contempt for bureaucracy is finely tuned after years of suffering under military leadership. The company of friends, proven under fire, is a powerful force shaping this effort to reintegrate.

Back at the memorial, the temperature dropped to zero. Our combined groups stood quietly in front of the stone monolith. Slim and somber, a man of thirty stepped toward the monument and turned to face the crowd. His black mustache moved up and down while a memorized speech plodded along in rhythm.

Peter took Sandy's arm. "He's not real Afgansty. Just politician."

Sandy confided. "It doesn't sound any better in translation."

Our group, standing off to the rear, gradually formed a small squad. Peter squeezed his new friend's arm.

"Bring your comrade, Sandy. Join us for eating tonight! You must meet some of our guys!"

Individuals from both groups paired up through an intuitive, matching process lasting for years after our trip. Peter and Nicolai collected us in front of the hotel. Unable to flag a taxi, we managed to crowd onto one of the always-full public buses.

The assigned female translator took the world's smallest elevator to Nicolai's apartment while we half-dozen comrades kicked the snow from our boots and climbed cement stairs to the fourth floor. Nicolai opened his front door with gusto.

"The housing office gives nine cubic meters per person when assigning space. Fortunately, I have two children!"

Fifteen people and a table stuffed the entire living room. After a feast of traditional foods and a numerous toasts with smoothly potent vodka, photos and stories came out. Nicolai's physical grace and disposition gave no clue that he had but one leg. With a big meal in our stomachs and happily lubricated with vodka, faces around the room blurred together into a snapshot of a happy family gathering, anywhere.

Our host pushed himself up from the table and addressed his captive and crowded audience. "As you know, we veterans are called Afgansty. Tonight you are present at the birth of a new word in the Russian language.

From now on, you Vietnam veterans will be known as "Vietnamsty!" Glasses charged, birth baptized.

Sandy leaned across to Peter. "You know, we have an expression now in our group. When we talk about our special Afgansty friend, we say, "Find your own Afgansty!'"

Peter choked on dessert, losing his composure. He laughed. "We say, "Stay away from my Vietnamsty!"

The room grew quiet as our translator asked Nicolai about his wounds and readjustment. And so began a story that will continue to be lived by veterans, from every generation, everywhere. Peter whispered that Nicolai was speaking, "soul to soul."

"This is our way of describing conversations such as this."

Nicolai continued. "You Vietnamsty have been where we have been, seen what we have seen, felt what we have felt. Almost as soon as we started to speak, you knew and identified with us. Language does not matter, different cultures do not matter, and different social backgrounds do not matter. We know you are brothers."

"We are back in the Soviet Union, but often our hearts and heads are not." Nicolai said. "When we sleep, we often see Afghanistan. We see our dead friends, we see the mountains and battle-fields there, we see our lives as soldiers there but when we tell people this, they don't want to hear, and some even become frightened and run away from us."

The small room was silent. Each man for a moment, remembering his own tour of duty, his own journey home. For the first time, many of the Afgansty vets said they felt another group understood the anxieties haunting them.

Public transportation stopped running at midnight, so the dinner party bundled up and threw a few snowballs while waiting for a local bus. Peter dug his hands into his coat pockets, staring up at the night. Sandy's arm went around Peter's shoulder. The younger man smiled. "When Russia get credit card, I get big car!"

Diary
Moscow to Alma Ata

Our flight lifted off in a snowstorm, everyone still wrestling with jet lag, and facing five more time zones. Entering the airport at Alma Ata, we met another circus. Twenty or so young men in uniform, complete with musical instruments, sang, hugged, and threw flowers. As television and movie crews hovered about, a circle of veterans from two wars, arm in arm, swayed to the rhythms of guitars and voices.

Buses delivered us to yet another feast and after the initial chaos, people paired up by magical happenstance, again to live happily ever after for the following week. Vodka appeared from purses, inside parkas and from under tables. Two former Blue Berets, Sergei and Zhenya, adopted Sandy and I.

Zhenya beamed. "We have Dan Quayles here too!" He had found a bureaucratic similarity shared by both countries. As in America, sons of high-ranking officials or well-connected families were not sent into combat.

Hotel Bar
Alma Ata, Kazakstan

American vets modeled a rap group for the Afgansty veterans. About thirty people sat in a circle in the friendly and familiar common ground of the hotel bar.

"Transparent Viet Cong were charging up our hill. I was alone at the top with all my friends dead, lying around me. The bullets from my rifle passed through the V.C. without effect, and just before they reached me...I woke up."

An excited Kazahk grabbed the wrist of our translator. An almost identical dream spilled out of him. Afgansty began to share feelings and problems, transforming the modeling into an authentic group therapy session. Our two delegations found common experiences in combat and a parallel universe upon returning home. Our circle became one group without borders or politics.

We moved into the dining room. Over some kind of mystery meat, Sergey and Zhenya confided that Soviet men most often express grief through song and visitation to a memorial or graveyard. A festive banquet can hit an emotional brick wall, when a song on the phonograph reminds celebrants of friends who didn't make it home.

Left-over tension from the rap group dissolved into good humor and appetite around our meal. One truly brave soul, volunteered for the dangerous mission of telling a joke. No small task when dealing with two cultures. Officer bashing seemed to be a safe topic.

"How many officers does it take to make a roof? It depends how thin you slice them!" Former enlisted men laughed and attacked everyone's recurring nightmare - the boiled potato.

A party member narrowed his eyes and in a conspiratorial tone asked, "Have you noticed the KGB agent following us?"

Sandy smiled, "Have you figured out which one of us is CIA?"

Two Afgansty standing nearby pointed to an American vodka victim sleeping at the end of the table, "Another government man on the job!"

Diary
Alma Ata, December

We made our way to a cluster of identical cement apartment houses surrounded by eight-story housing projects that made up Zhenya's neighborhood. When his front door opened, our senses were overwhelmed by voices, delicious odors, and the overzealous Soviet central heating.

The light in the window of the Russian soul reveals a kitchen and sitting room. Blazing with color, eyes feast on a smorgasbord of clutter, rich in diversity and personal history. No color-coordinated themes here, no fashion statement, only a mother's home, overpopulated with mementos, memories, and knick-knacks, displayed with some inscrutable sense of order. Stripping away coats, hats, scarves, and boots like so many layers of mask required in the severe social climate outside, we entered sanctuary.

The vitality and passion, so much a part of the Soviet character, are reined in while outside of private homes. With friends and family gathered in happy conspiracy, sitting rooms illuminate the spirit and release the energy saved for expression in the true socialist republic, the home.

Irena and Marianna had been shopping for days, standing in long lines to prepare a banquet for the guests of their husbands. Mountains of food demanded to be eaten in compliance with Southern hospitality. Bottles of Georgian wine, vodka, and champagne were lined up like good soldiers, waiting to do their duty.

Sergey stood apart, smoking a cigarette on the balcony with Sandy. "A man can lose his children and make others, he can lose his wife and get another but when he loses a best friend, he is gone forever."

Empty bottles stood at ease, their duty done. Irena emerged from the kitchen and told the toastmasters to knock it off; reminding us it was time for the last bus. Hugs and Soviet man kisses sent is out into the snow.

Eight days in Alma Ata were filled with tours, workshops, home visits, solo adventures, and plenty of good memories for everyone. Yet one member of the Afgansty group was missing...

Diary
Alma Ata People's Hospital

Outside the service entrance to the hospital, fog surrounded three men hovering about a small red sedan. Cement walls stared down and for a moment, we two Americans felt like criminals of the State. Someone was watching from somewhere, only allowing the drama to continue in the hope of entrapping more conspirators.

Sergey had been in the hospital now for ten or twelve minutes. Taking no chances, the car engine was running, and our getaway team paced the driveway trying to stay warm. Zhenya smoked while Sandy and I laughed nervously about the possible consequences of kidnapping a patient from the Alma Ata Peoples' Hospital. "Siberia! Sodium pentothal! Hard labor! Boiled potatoes!" Gruesome penalties indeed.

Sasha snuck out of the back door of the amputee wing with a paper bag of clothes. His friend had sworn to leave the hospital in time to meet with Vietnamsty who had come all the way to Alma Ata. This was his last chance.

115

Clanging metal doors burst open onto the loading dock. A crutch under each arm, blond hair crowning the victory smile of a boy playing hooky, Sasha looked down on his new comrades. Behind him, Sasha leaned against the door, nodding: a clean getaway.

The crutches stepped forward, Sasha's body followed. He no longer had legs. Heavy metal and leather limbs swung stiffly, leaving railroad tracks in the snow. He pulled to a stop in front of Sandy and me and reached out to hold us both in his iron grip.

We five vets squeezed into Zhenya's rusting sedan and roared off, challenging pedestrians all the way to Sasha's apartment. With no elevator, Sasha was the last one to join his homecoming on the second floor.

A well-dressed and sophisticated woman showed us into her sitting room. Oriental rugs, handsome furnishings, full bookshelves, and stereo components reflected the successful career of Sasha's wife, Lena, an assistant director of city planning.

Strength and feminine grace flowed from Lena as she attended to her husband's guests. The mutual love and respect and her pleasure in his homecoming felt like the presence of another person in the room.

Afgansty lyrics came to life out of the stereo. This now familiar music had become an overture from our ritual of sharing. After a toast with homemade vodka, Sasha opened his photo album. Lena, perhaps lamenting the continuing presence and celebration of war in her home, rose, and excused herself.

She studied these men who were still willing to feel good about their combat experiences, reminiscing over her coffee table, creating a new ritual she must play hostess to for years to come. Her husband sat propped up by pillows, again with brothers and new friends who understood him in a way she never could or ever wanted to. Lena turned and walked into her kitchen.

Sasha and I were alone on the couch, the others off to recruit a replacement for the now empty bottle of vodka.

He dealt his snapshots onto the table and identified friends and wartime circumstances. With identical memories and images, no translation was necessary. No language can describe such a moment.

My arm resting gently across the former commando's shoulders, I felt the pride and affection Sasha still held for his army career and comrades. Black-and-white memories covered the coffee table in front of us. Sasha became very still and gazed into a large color portrait on his lap. There, in full dress uniform, a decorated officer and leader of men in his prime...stood Sasha.

Captivated, he breathed in slowly, deeply. His full chest pushed him back into the couch, holding him erect. Turning to me, his soul full upon his face, he said with his heart, "Yes. This is the way I really am."

Quietly, involuntarily, Sasha's breath escaped, emptying him completely. With a small shrug, his smile returned and he looked down again at the photo he held in his hands. Reaching over the table, he dropped it face down on the pile of friends who hadn't made it home.

Another tray of food floated around the corner, followed by Lena. Her buoyant step hesitated as she felt the subtle change in her husband. Sasha lifted his head and squared his shoulders, once again becoming the attentive and cheerful host.

"We need room for tray!" Lena announced, and bent down over the coffee table. Gathering the photographs into their shoebox, she returned them to their closet, buried again, out of sight.

Diary
Farewell Party
Moscow

Peter Tamarov coordinated the farewell supper for American Vietnamsty. At the end of the evening he toasted the combined group and families. "Afghanistan is our Christ! We must make him easy in our heart...just as with your own Christ - Vietnam. When we see real Afghanistan in our minds - we must find positive memory!"

The farewell banquet was over and the last Afgansty speaker rose with a translator. "Socially and emotionally your visit has been a success. We will never forget the brotherhood and hope you have brought into our veterans' clubs and personal lives."

118

Diary
Moscow Airport

I asked Peter if he was aware of any eccentric behavior on the part of the Vietnamsty. He nodded. "Of course! We have eyes! We can match your men with our friends who act the same. To see your still-wounded men makes us work harder on these issues. We do not want to be the same in twenty years!"

Our new friends grew silent when the return flight to Copenhagen was announced. Photos, speeches, gifts, addresses scribbled, a last bear hug, kisses, a wave, Russia retreated into the distance, a chapter full of hope and promise for both Afgansty and Vietnamsty.

SAS Flight 743

Sandy caressed his first decent beer in three weeks as the jumbo jet climbed to cruising altitude. At his elbow, a New Age veteran asked for a vegetarian entree. Sandy took advantage of the captive audience, strapped in next to him.

"There was seduction in believing what we were doing was serious in a self-validating, egoistic kind of way. But the Afgansty and external events kept us honest. I suspect that we nineteen vets have very different stories to tell. It's probably like the story of the blind men touching a different part of the elephant." His neighbor was still awake and not complaining so Sandy continued.

"The role of older brother seems to be the best way to describe our relationship with the Afgansty, and we spent a lot of time listening and learning from them at one point. There was consensus that we were learning more from them than they from us. They taught us about the meaning of ritual, visits to the cemetery, and singing war ballads together. They taught us about community. I feel the interpersonal isolation of the Afgansty is much less than that of Vietnam veterans. After all, many of them grew up together and are now helping each other get well."

Staring at the ceiling in the cabin, he added a caption. "If you strip away all the non-essentials, these people are you and me with the same hopes and desires. The enemies are the groups and governments who conspire to divide us."

The jet leveled off and Sandy closed his eyes, seeing again the farewell party as Soviets and Americans, interchangeable and indistinguishable, raised their glasses. "May our children know moments such as this!"

The ringing of twelve glasses sounded as one.

In February of 1988, the California-based Vietnam Restoration Project sent their first team of twelve Vietnam veterans back to "help build that which they had helped to destroy." A medical clinic was built in the seacoast town of Vung Tau. This was the first in an ongoing program to build public service structures in Vietnam. The value of reconstruction projects is a therapeutic healing process for Soviets, Americans and the citizens of the countries affected by war.

After the Soviet pullout from Afghanistan, a small group of Afgansty received permission from both countries to return as civilians. Peter Tamarov led a group of Afgansty combat veterans to rebuild an apartment complex destroyed by Soviet gunfire some years before. Many of these volunteers had been stationed in the same town during their tour of duty.

PART FOUR

The Soviet trip deepened my understanding of PTSD. I had traveled nine-thousand miles to Moscow before meeting with American veterans, people with identical wartime experiences, feelings, and readjustment issues. Back in the States, these brothers-in-arms helped me navigate the maze of Veterans Administration red tape and receive assistance. Group and individual therapy followed; both good and bad, assholes and angels.

While both combatants and civilians often present life-long symptoms, it is possible through education to change responses to feelings and situations triggering episodes. Although I worked for years with South Vietnamese Army veterans and their many challenges as refugees, I always provided services and seldom imagined that I too, needed help. Continuing employment in the social service industry focused on the client and postponed any need to look at my own symptoms; transience, trust, and the inability to imagine a future.

For the current generation of returning veterans, how-to-heal manuals, books, retreats, workshops, advocates, consultants, vet clinics, a streamlined VA program, on-line chat communities, and media coverage are all part of the growing PTSD industry. It's not enough. Already, increased rates of suicide, homelessness, divorce, and unemployment plague our troops, returning from the Middle East and Afghanistan.

In the decades following my tour of duty, I developed a pattern for coping. Successful moments of readjustment and routine normal life were followed by anxiety and flight. Predictable daily schedules triggered visceral memory of ambush and impending disaster. Episodes of transience, wandering, and misadventures punctuated respectable positions in social service advocacy serving ex-cons, immigrants, refugees, low-income communities, third world countries, Native Americans, and two tours with the Peace Corps.

Survivors of trauma can often recognize one other and often find solace in socializing. Some sort of intuitive connection drove my decision making process and as a staff member of an agency, program, or institution, I believed I was guiding, helping, and yes, even saving other survivors. Boundaries got fuzzy. Emotionally disturbed vets, brown and yellow people became my community.... just like the war.

The routine lives of suburban families began to hold some appeal and I arrived spontaneously on the doorstep of my oldest friend. As adult men who bonded during the teenage years often do, we hugged and years of estrangement dissolved. With a wife, five children, a big ranch-style home and a great career as a salesman, he had created everything I walked away from: the American Dream.

A few nights later, alone in the back yard, he asked, "If I disappeared, will you stay around and help out with the kids?"

Shocked, I could only say, "Cancer?"

He shook his head and stared at the fire inside the big stainless steel barbecue.

"I can't stand all this anymore. I'm thinking of driving to the desert and disappearing."

Boy was I cured. He was fantasizing about my lifestyle and perceived freedom. I left Thousand Oaks, California, feeling much better about running around the planet and seeking out interesting experiences.

Sometimes, the experience found me...

Reunion!

Long Beach, CA

1989

"Ron! How the hell did you find my number?"

He sounded the same; calm, in control, distant...

"Well, I went to a neighborhood Christmas party last night. Some of us were talking in the kitchen about Vietnam. After a while and a couple of drinks, well Mac, your high school girlfriend was there. Small world."

"Jesus."

"Don't worry, she's still married."

"I wondered if you made it back, Ron. I saw the tracer go through your foot."

"Got medivaced the next day. It was either stay there with you and die or run for it. But you made it, too."

Silence

"Why don't you fly down here and spend the weekend? We have a lot to talk about. I'll send you a ticket."

My first reunion with a Fox Company buddy; brotherhood, survivors, Semper Fi!

"OK!"

It was dark when we met at the John Wayne Airport in Southern California. Ron was a little heavier and still in uniform.

"Hey, Brother!" My hug seemed to embarrass him. "What's the badge?"

"County Sherriff, air support, I ride shot gun on night assist chopper, you know, spot light, loud speaker, but no weapons though. In fact, I'm on stand-by and got called in. Our hanger's across the tarmac. You got back seat tonight."

What a flash-back; twenty two years with no contact, up in a chopper, and after the bad guys. Was Ron still fighting the war? A lot of vets went into law enforcement – or crime, kind of a lateral transfer. An hour later we were five-hundred feet over some low income neighborhood. Ron's spotlight followed a naked woman running down a sidewalk,

He turned around. "High on crack, Looks like the patrol unit has her cornered."

The chopper elevated and headed east, waiting for another call. It didn't take long.

"Mac, we got a hold up in a bar down there with hostages. They want us to light up the roof so he doesn't climb up and run across the tops of adjacent buildings."

And so it went for three hours. Another crew took over after we landed and Ron drove us in his Imperial to his home in Long Beach.

"Wow, this is beautiful, Ron."

"My wife and I put everything we have into it. She's a stewardess and on an overnight. You can wash up out there in the pool house. Scotch?"

"Good to see you, Ron."

"Uh, yeah. I'll be in the den."

Soon, we were sitting in a paneled den, full of Marine Corps memorabilia. After his second Scotch, Ron began to relax. "You got kids Mac?"

"Yes, a wonderful daughter."

He looked over at one of the many pictures of him and his wife on the oak desk. "We don't. Decided to focus on ourselves and a flexible life style." He held up the bottle. "I'm having one more. You?"

"No thanks." Why did I feel like I was interviewing for a job?

Ron sipped his double. "What happened to you on Union II?"

Was this it? Were we going to bond now? "Didn't think I was gonna make it, Ron. Stayed out all night and somehow brought back nine guys. I found a radio and Connerly guided us back in to where survivors had set a perimeter."

He stared at the memorabilia on the wall behind me. "You get a medal?"

"Yeah, nothin much."

The glass went down on his desk. "We both went forward, nobody else did. You know what happened, Mac. Looked like we were the next to die out there. I ran back to cover and you chose not to."

What was up? We both knew exactly what happened: damned if you ran, damned if you stayed. "That's right."

He stood and walked over to wall and straightened one of the frames. I looked around. There was an empty spot in the middle. "Mac, I want you to write a recommendation for me."

"For what?"

"I need proof that I went out there with you to help the wounded so I can get my commendation. They will issue one if you submit collaboration for my statement."

Jesus Christ. This was why he contacted me. It was only Friday night. My plane didn't leave until Sunday. Fuck.

"Ron, I'll take that drink,"

Veterans All
Marin County, CA
1993

"What is a resume, Mister Mac?"

He was better dressed than his English, much more elegant than I. I handed him a folder.

"Here is an example. This person just got a job in San Francisco as an interpreter in the public schools. You can use that typewriter over there."

He stood gracefully and pressed his hands together in prayer. "Thank you, Mister Mac."

Our local satellite office of the Center for Southeast Asian Resettlement and Redevelopment held staff from five countries. My graduate degree, Vietnamese language, and gift for common sense deposited me behind a desk, finding jobs for refugees. Each day drama, comedy, and tragedy paraded through my office. What next?

The phone rang.

"That you, Mac?"

"Hi Cheng."

"You know the Vietnamese Trade Association is presenting products over in Frisco, right?" Always soft, his voice carried a subtle tone of intrigue. He knew how to work me.

"Yeah. You want to go?"

"Already did. Met a delegate who speaks Chinese and he wants to talk to you."

Cheng had the Chinese nose for profit and a refugee's flexibility with legal matters.

"OK. Bring him to my house for lunch. "

"We are in my car now. He must return by two. No photos."

"See you there. You know where the key is."

This was gonna be good…

"Here is my resume, Mister Mac."

"You finished already, Tangen? "

He stood waiting as I read it over. "Says here, you have been a military general, businessman, yak herdsman, caravan master, and a slave. You look pretty young to have such a long work history."

He nodded. "These are jobs from my past lives. In this life I have been a monk and a teacher."

By then, my experiences with other cultures taught me to expect anything, so I kept a straight face, but I couldn't wait to tell the guys later down at the saloon.

"Tangen, the Berkeley Seminary is looking for a cultural informant and translator. I will set up an interview."

Trying to hide his pleasure, he bowed and floated out the way he came in.

Cheng had parked in my space so I pulled up on the lawn. Small, even for a Vietnamese, our guest stood when I entered. He wore the standard uniform of long sleeved white shirt and black slacks, both one size too big. A shoebox lay in the center of the kitchen table.

Cheng lubricated the introductions with hot tea, sliced orange sections, and his usual charm. "Mr. Tu requests his identity remain secret during negotiations."

For what?

"He knows you fought in the war, are a friend of all soldiers, and know many people in Washington D.C."

I did? What was Cheng up to?

I smiled, nodded and sat down at Marin County's first negotiation with a man from the only country to defeat the United States in war.

Mr. Tu spoke to Cheng in a southern Chinese dialect. "He says he hopes to be your neighbor after he is granted political asylum. The weather reminds him of Hanoi."

The shoebox seemed to swell and grow larger. Cheng raised his eyebrows and asked a question. Tu reached across the table and lifted off the lid of the box. Fake Nikes? Stolen Rolexes?

Only a small packet wrapped in Chinese silk.

I got that old feelin'. The past lay there like a bad dream that just wouldn't go away. This time the nightmare was nicely packaged in red silk: the Chinese symbol for lucky money.

Tu slowly rolled out the fabric with delicate fingers which no doubt set booby traps not too long ago. He spread out four items and sat back in his chair.

Apparently, he had memorized one English sentence. "Two million dollar, Mister Mac. Some you, some Cheng Lim."

Looking back at me from my kitchen table, four souvenirs from Vietnam: dog tags, a hand written letter, an old photo, and a severed finger. In those days we all knew of the standing reward for evidence proving the existence of a live POW.

Cheng shattered my trance. "Mr. Tu will be here with the trade mission until Saturday. We may keep these things as proof of a POW but you must not reveal his identity even after sanctuary is granted. Communist cadre came into Northern California concealed in the second wave of immigration."

Jesus! I probably got some of them jobs. "OK, Tu. I know someone." But who?

He relaxed for the first time and sipped some tea, his two hands around an Asian cup with no finger loop. Staring out the front window, he scanned the houses on my street, no doubt seeing himself with a new family living on an American street of gold.

Cheng looked at his watch and nodded in the direction of the Golden Gate Bridge. The bounty hunter and I stood up and walked to the door. "Chao Anh, Ong Mac."

"Chao Anh, Ong Tu."

From the porch, I watched the pickup truck pull away. Ripples of our war spread across time and touched us as it always would.

My house held no memorabilia on the walls, no photos of Marine buddies in an album, no uniform hanging in the back of the closet and no medals stashed in the back of a dresser drawer. What did I have? Total immersion in the refugee community as a job counselor for South Vietnamese Army vets, housing agent for elderly refugees and a Vietnamese girlfriend.

Every day I witnessed the Southeast Asian international resettlement games: Catholic vs. Buddhist, North vs. South, educated vs. villager, nationalist vs. royalist, and all the variations. Fate had placed me in the role of codependent, confidant, and sometimes co-conspirator as new arrivals sought out a sympathetic power broker and advocate, matching their own cultural model .

I looked over at the severed finger on the table. Now what? Maybe Ben Johnson was over at the bar lecturing to tourists. I picked up the phone.

Judy answered, "He's gone home, thank God!"

Twenty minutes later I left Inverness behind and headed north for Johnson's Oyster Ranch on nearby Tomales Bay. Old trailers, doublewides, funky sheds, and a funky retail storefront stood like a backdrop from a hillbilly movie.

Surrounded by dairy and cattle ranches of the original Portuguese, Italian, and Irish homesteads, strings of cultivated oysters hovered in cold waters. Up on the porch, Ben sat in his throne: an old wicker chair with wings on each side. Lieutenant Numbnuts, his bodyguard lay next to him on his porch. He didn't have to bark. Ben took care of that job.

Through a flattened and often-broken nose he snorted, "What'd you want?"

During our first encounter in the Western Saloon he "made" me as a combat vet. I too felt that special affinity and our intimacy grew over both beers and time. Was I the only one who knew? All his stories were true.

Too many years in covert and black operations had wounded him deeply, and there would be no return for Ben from the shadows. A mask of cynicism hid a heart of gold as he played town drunk. Beer and isolation kept the shadow demons on the other side of the concertina wire. Both of us the same age, he looked twenty years older.

Ben believed in an America that no longer existed. He championed the underdog, smuggled and employed illegal aliens from three countries, contributed to homeless shelters, and bought drinks for any and all. His bayside business was worth a million and a half.

I looked around the oyster camp. A couple of heads popped out of the window in the shucking shack where I taught English on Thursday nights. Always hyper-vigilant, employees knew much more English than they showed.

"Ben, you still have a contact in the Pentagon?"

He read my concern and placed his beer down on top of the cooler.

"Why?"

"Can we go inside?"

"Follow me." Never as drunk as he pretended, we navigated a minefield of empties and entered the trailer with Lt. Numbnuts trailing behind.

A card table stood in the kitchen area and soon held two Budweisers. "Sit down. OK. Whatya got?"

I pushed aside a bag of Cheetos and dropped the packet on the table. Ben pulled out bifocals, sat up straight and opened the silk. The finger spilled out, rolled around a bit and lay there, pointing at him.

He reached into pile on the counter and pulled out a magnifying glass. "Finger print is long gone. What else is in here?"

His own past appeared and laid there like three tombstones: dog tags, a letter, and a photo. A Filipino employee in my class had whispered, "Mr. Ben, he prisoner in communist camp, Mindanao. Very bad!"

He read the letter while the finger still pointed his way. Curmudgeon, cynic, and tough old bird, Ben Johnson laid his head down on the table and cried. Lt. Numbnuts whined, rose up and put his head in Ben's lap, standing guard until this most recent assault from the past faded.

A minute passed. Unashamed, Ben wiped his nose with the bag of Cheetos. "This way."

His bedroom held a strange mix of Asian art, carved knick-knacks, old photos, bookshelves full of philosophy, classical literature, a half finished oil canvas on an easel tripod, and a huge pile of gold Krugerrrands on top of the dresser. Stacked against the wall, and next to a bed that hadn't been made since the Battle of Hue City, stood three rifles, all clean and shiny, all converted to full automatic.

In the far corner, Ben picked up an old circular dial phone and pulled the cylinder all the way round. "Operator, I want to place a collect call to the Pentagon. 7036971776, General Xxxx. Tell him it's Ben Johnson."

He looked back at me and wiggled a finger. Was this really happening? I moved to his side. Behind me, Lt. Numbnuts growled.

"Yes, General, it's Ben. Fine, thank you Sir. General I have a man here with some Intel on a possible POW. I can vouch for him."

He turned and pushed the receiver at me.

"Hello General."

"What have you got, son?" He sounded like a general.

I described the contents of the packet and how they came to be in my possession.

The man in the Pentagon was not impressed. "Yes. These types of submissions are more frequent now that travel to Vietnam has been loosened up. Photograph everything and send it to me. Ben has the address. And tell that sonofabitch commie gook to get a photo of our POW holding next week's copy of the International Times available in Vietnam. Then we're on to something. Now give me Ben."

"Yes Sir."

I needed a beer so I returned to the kitchen, sat back down at the card table, and grabbed a cold one from the cooler. Lt. Numbnuts stared at me from the bedroom, keeping score.

Ben dropped a business card on the table. "Here's the address for the photos. Give it back after you send the stuff." Four stars stood in formation under a D.C. address. "And don't say a damn word."

"OK Ben." I tossed down the rest of the Budweiser. "I gotta get this stuff back to the trade rep."

He pulled a dusty photo off the wall and stared at small squad of guerilla fighters. "We taught those gook assholes good."

He opened another beer and toasted the photo. "Now you're sellin' our memories."

Cursed by my tribe,
if I forgive him.
The Merchant of Venice
Shakespeare

Second Homecoming
Nong Son, Vietnam
1999

After 32 years, 6500 miles, 3 airplanes, and 4 hours in a rusty Russian sedan, familiar rice paddies and tree lines appear alongside a wide brown river. Mopeds and a few more people roam the frontage road, yet this fertile valley is almost unchanged in the photo album of my mind.

Our car slows, stops. I'm here. Standing on the sandy shore of the Thu Bon, I stare across the wide river at the village of Nong Son and into yesterday. Why have I returned after all these years?

Rich Hoffman and I set out on May 5 of this year to recapture Vietnam. Our tour of duty will be three weeks. This time we are tourists heavily armed with dollars. Four years of working with Vietnamese refugees in California, and my role as a Marine interpreter left me with positive cross-cultural experiences and memories. How bad could it be?

Nine long months in the infantry and the Marine Corps sent me to live alone in the village of Nong Son. My role as an English teacher and liaison with the South

Vietnamese militia would require winning the support of villagers. It was hoped I might be supplied with intelligence to fight the Viet Cong in Quang Nam Province.

Now only Asian profiteers in search of hardwood forests venture this deep into the interior. As we travel along the back roads, wonder and humor on the faces of farmers working in the paddies stare back at us. Most rural Vietnamese look at tourists with frank curiosity and respond smile for smile.

The dignity found in these traditional communities replaces the city hustlers, beggars and vendors. Blond, physically fit, and dressed in Tae Kwan Do attire, Rich draws a small crowd each time we exit the car.

In the mountains now we are swept away by lush and sensual memories pulling us into the past; the harsh perfume of noontime cooking fires, bright conical hats floating over green rice fields, sing-song voices bargaining raw meat, sweat and humidity- all mix together melting away the years. My feet want to walk down the middle of a rice paddy. Are the adrenaline rush and paranoia still there just under the surface?

Nong Son village stands at the bottom of a eighteen-hundred-foot hill. White, blue, and green colonial French buildings in orderly rows still survive, saluting the patience of the Vietnamese in three wars of liberation. Our Marine security company once ran patrols from here and commanded the valley with mortars placed on top of the hill. Military historians would later characterize the Marine defense of Vietnam's only working coal mine as 'symbolic' with acceptable losses.

The same ferryman from years ago approaches. Thin and brown moving in slow rhythm, it's hard to distinguish arms and legs from his pole and long-handled rudder. He smiles as he did so long ago, but now his ancient skull strains against leathery skin impatient for its turn. He poles the boat closer to shore.

Rich, our interpreter Mr. Chin and I climb in. Carved from a tree trunk, the long slender canoe glides across the murky water and into the past. For many Marines this would become The River Styx.

Drifting across the silky brown Thu Bon I gaze downriver. Once, we won the hearts and filled the pocketbooks of fishermen by dropping grenades to stun fish and bringing them to the surface. Later, the same fishing boats dropped us at launch points for patrols or ambushes into the valley.

Gently, the canoe touches the opposite shore. We step out and onto the soil of Nong Son. I'm here. I'm back, and for a moment, young again. It's 1967. I'm stepping off the metal ferryboat that conveys my platoon into Nong Son on July 1. Then I carried seventy pounds on top of a flak jacket. Today I am sweating with a light rucksack and tee shirt. I look down expecting to see jungle boots and watch tennis shoes sink into the red mud.

Can I find my old plaster house? Is the classroom still intact? Will the students now middle aged, recognize me? So many happy memories in the midst of war and chaos: Vietnamese writing pen pal letters to my old high school, medical treatment for villagers, Marine vs. villagers in volley ball and soccer, intimate and clandestine discussions of war, politics and ethics in our secluded classroom and ultimately, my acceptance into this remote village near the Cambodian border.

Our small group approaches the first buildings. Army officers in the same gray-green wartime uniforms and pith helmets step out onto the veranda and gesture to us to climb up the stone stairs. A red metal star flashes from a belt buckle.

Our charming and effervescent Mr. Chin suddenly becomes passive, obedient. Directed to enter a small office, we sit around a small circular table with the officers standing above, staring down. We wait. A cross-cultural standoff. Overhead, a tired fan slices through afternoon heat. Who are we? The hotel has our passports. Phone calls are made. Thirty-minutes pass. Hyper-vigilant, Rich scans the mood, exits, and river below. Identities verified. Why are we here? To visit my wartime station. No American has ever returned here. Nong Son is not on the official tourist list. More phone calls. This time to Hanoi.

Mr. Chin does his best to lubricate the tension in the room, but he is in deep water and obviously afraid. Slowly curiosity wins out over suspicion and boredom. When will these men stationed in such an isolated region get a chance like this again? Tea and cigarettes are presented. I place a box of American Marlboros on the table. Mr. Chin finally relaxes and begins to translate capitalism into communism.

I sip perhaps the strongest tea ever poured. As a foreign invader and former occupier of Nong Son, the army personnel are interested in my experiences and perspective. Hoping to retrieve my story without providing any information of their own, they begin to gently probe. More employees and troops collect in the windows and doorway. We are yesterday come back, tall pale ghosts haunting those old enough to remember.

The Vietnamese officials are concerned that I may understand their conversation. Vietnamese is a tonal language and my ear of out of tune. Most of it passes by and blends with the squeaking of the fan overhead. Captain Kiet asks what intelligence I was able to collect while an operative school teacher. Humor seems the best choice. "I was both young and stupid and found out only one thing! I liked teaching and it has been my career." Laughter. They appreciate evasion.

Captain Kiet feels more comfortable. He smiles, keeping his hand on my forearm. I remember adult male students walking home and holding hands with me along the street outside this same window. Scary the first time. He suggests that we may be able to stroll along the frontage road and walk ten meters into the village.

Am I man enough to hold hands?

Mr. Chin exhales. He may earn his bonus yet. We rise, march down the steps and head into the ville. Over there is the volleyball court where Marines beat the villagers. Adjacent is the soccer field where the Vietnamese ran circles around the taller, heavier Americans. Behind the playing field is the classroom where students thrilled to my nonexistent teaching skills.

The Nong Son coalmine is now a government-run and army-administered operation. The entire former population was relocated after the War of Liberation. A few of the stucco buildings received new paint, but all the landmarks, buildings and huts stand there exactly as they did in 1967. Few returning American veterans will find such a moment. Most former US sites suffered fates similar to our old battalion base at An Hoa. A name change in 1975 was not enough. An Hoa is now underwater as the result of new dam construction.

Nong Son. Where are the former children and adults? Both taught me how to reclaim my humanity in the middle of the killing fields. They are scattered now, just like the Marines once stationed on Nong Son Hill, each completing their own destiny. For many, their lives ended on patrol, others as "collateral damage" or at midnight July 4, 1967 as VC overran the hilltop.

Captain Kiet takes my hand and leads me to a side street and walks us uphill half a block. We peek around the corner and I see my old plaster apartment attached to the end of a row of identical units. My room, where we had a Halloween party and bobbed for mangoes, where adults cried when I translated letters from their American pen pals. My room, where I wrote letters to the parents of dead friends from Foxtrot Company. Is my journal still buried under the floor? I'd like to read the thoughts and feelings of the young man I used to be.

As we walk back the way we came I hand Captain Kiet a small package of a dozen "exotic" American vegetable and fruit seeds. "My friend. These are from my family to your family. When I come back next year, I want some rutabaga pudding."

Looking at the picture of a rutabaga on the seed packet, he shakes his head and then laughs. We stop and stare up at the top of Nong Son Hill where Foxtrot was overrun. Who won? Brutality.

"Mr. Mac, I apologize your old friends not here." Captain Kiet is sad for the first time, thinking perhaps also of lost comrades. The two of us stand with one foot in the past and another in the moment. He brings us back to the present.

"Perhaps we have new friend today."

Coming down the road is a dignified and well-dressed man of fifty. He is hard to read but the news he carries cannot be good. Captain Kiet assumes his official persona. "Mr. Mac, I introduce you Mr. Kinh. He fight against your group top of hill. He last one here living."

Mr. Kinh's eyes bore into me. I want to share a beer, discuss battle tactics, small-unit action and personal survival. Healing, reconciliation, a psychic cease-fire. You know, like on 60 Minutes.

This former freedom fighter feels something far different. Polite and stiffly formal, he offers his hand but there is no connection. There are only two men reaching across the years, each with old wounds, some yet to heal.

Offended I have returned a second time Mr. Kinh turns and walks back into his village, his people, and his own past.

Minutes later the canoe leaves the shore and I look over my shoulder. Nong Son is still there, different now but forever the same. In midstream, I pull papers from my rucksack and read the lists one last time. In my hands are the names of all the Foxtrot Marines killed in action; one hundred and forty-two. Gently, lovingly, I tear the papers into many pieces and release them to the waters of the Thu Bon.

Back now in Hawaii, my skin is brown from the sun over Quang Nam Province, and the red mud of Vietnam is still on my shoes. I live quietly at the end of town beside a river. It's muddy most of the time. Some nights when the wind blows down from the mountain and rain beats a rhythm on the broad leaves outside my window, I hear again that dark music from another time, another place.

PTSD QUARTET

I
Emotional Hygiene
Marin County, CA
Ongoing…

Even now, this very moment, I feel it. A flash back? Hyper-vigilance? Distrust? Fear of crowds? Need for isolation?

No.

Wouldn't it be great if it *were* just something mental? A pill, a drink, or a doobie could fix it, at least for a little while. But on my deathbed, my old friend will whisper, "Still here."

We were animals back then, taking turns with the enemy: Predator. Hunted. Predator. Both sides miserable, exhausted, wet or hot, soaked or dehydrated, dirty, thin, and filthy. If we lived long enough we devolved and sank into the jungle of the sixth sense, an expanded aura constantly feeling and filtering the atmosphere around us for danger and death.

During our war, hygiene was impossible for full-time combatants. Shaving, showers, shampooing, all these little pleasures ordinarily taken for granted were not only infrequent but inadequate. A swim in the Thu Bon River without soap and protected by heavily armed companions was the highlight of the month.

Our feet, armpits, and crotch, targeted by insects, leeches, diseases, and discomfort, ached for treatment and relief. A powder or cream from Doc, our medic, helped for a few hours, then slowly, inevitably, rice paddy, forest, or jungle once again worked its dark magic on foreign bodies.

As time passed a singular obsession developed: What one part of my body could be kept clean daily? What bit of sanitary sanity connecting me back home with The World could I defend and save from the overwhelming assault of The Bush?

The answer came roaring in on the weekly resupply chopper. Red and I were trading cans from C-rations at lunch when the H34 arrived at our outpost on Phu Loc Six.

Red's mother, warned of supply scavengers who "supported" us from safe areas, always sent two separate boxes. Support personnel soon learned to let one package slip through and kept the other one as payment. This time, they must have been drinking or stoned. Red opened two identical packages.

"Hey Mac." He spread out the latest treasures from Mom. "I got two manicure kits here. You want one."

I stopped chewing. "Let me see."

"You got two bags of chocolate, Red. What you gonna do with those?"

He stuffed both bags of Hershey Kisses into an empty ammo can.

"Eat this." He tossed a small leather sack and it landed in my C-rat box.

The zipper slid open easily. Inside, laid out and ready for inspection, a fingernail tool kit; half a dozen little items to trim, clean, and cut nails and cuticles. Shining brightly, a long slender blade sparkled in the tropical sun. I pushed it out of its collar and inspected for sharpness. Why not?

I held the backs of my hands out in front of me and examined my fingers. The ten-member squad stood at attention. Little black berets of dirt on top of each blank face.

Long accustomed to non-intervention, the mud, red dirt, and rice paddy feces challenged me from under the middle fingernail. Black, thick, and a quarter inch deep, a dark crescent moon helmet crowned the wrinkled finger below. Three months of neglect and fermentation had given birth to a formidable foe.

It took ten days.

By the time we left the outpost and saddled up for rotation back to base camp, I was sure snipers would spot the sparkle off my shiny fingernails. Engineers swept the trail ahead for booby traps, and off we went. Everything felt the same as usual: hyper- vigilance, free-floating anxiety, and paranoia. Yet this time something different vibrated.

My fingernails were sending me messages! "We're clean!" I must admit it was a bit distracting at first; ten little transmitters blasting away with a clear signal.

Yet the overall affect was reassuring. No matter what might happen in the chaos of combat, part of me transcended the filth of The Bush. I had control.

Over the next few weeks the messages became more subtle and differentiated. "Not clean. Getting dirty. Filthy. Pay attention!" So I did. We had an agreement, and when neglected on my part, the signal grew in strength, and insomnia was the price. And so it went, monsoon, heat, dust, and through-out the nights. I felt clean. Part of me was "not there," and somehow… safe.

The messages have never stopped broadcasting. A moment ago I stopped typing to drag a nail file through dirt accumulated from gardening… yes, I had to.

Twenty years after the war, my therapist asked, "Does it make you think of Vietnam when your fingernails talk to you?"

I looked down at my old friends. "Doc, when they stop, its time to commit me."

II
"It Ain't My Fault!"
Marin County, CA
Ongoing...

"Hey. These handcuffs are cutting into my wrists."

"Sorry, they're the new plastic ones. Sit tight back there. We're almost to the county jail."

The back seat of the Sheriff's patrol car was not built for comfort. Thick transparent seat covers installed for queasy drunks provided little cushion, so I sat up straight to take the pressure off my hands, locked behind me.

The deputy was a decent sort. "Have you ever received psychiatric treatment or been hospitalized for mental problems? Don't lie to me. I'm running a background check on you right now. You seem like a reasonable guy. How'd you ever get into a mess like this?"

I leaned back and thought for a second, How did this happen...?

Oh yeah. The Viet Cong. It was their fault, still extracting revenge and reparation after thirty-five years. In vivid flashback, I saw sand-bag bunkers and the metal airstrip at An Hoa. Gunny Jones had us standing tall out in front of Fox Company hooches.

"OK you Shitbirds, you're issued one standard packet of Rit Dye, color: Forest Green. At 1800, you will be back here in formation with your skivvies: displayed, dry, and dyed fuckin green! And you all know why! Some

151

fuckin' retard general in Da Nang had another brilliant fuckin' idea."

I tried not to look at Rabbi, who was scratching his butt. Wounds itched when healing, and Rabinowitz just got back from the infirmary after a week of lying on his stomach. A sniper got him as 2nd Platoon took a break on a sweep down by the river.

Rabbi wandered off, squatted down to crap in the rice paddy just like a villager, and over his shoulder yelled, "This kosher manure will help out big time."

Young green plants blended with his dirty green fatigues and helmet. Everything went as planned until he dropped trou. Hanging out there for every sniper in Vietnam to see was a big white bull's eye in the field of green. Cowboy had to crawl out and drag him back while the platoon fired randomly into the distant tree line.

Rabbi had joined the growing number of ass wounded grunts, a statistic passed up to decision makers at the Imperial Hotel in Da Nang, no doubt during happy hour.

The following day and wearing newly dyed underwear we saddled up and with sixty pounds of gear and left base camp for the long walk to Nong Son Hill. Hot and humid, we were soaked in sweat before losing sight of perimeter at An Hoa.

Two hours later, we crowded onto a metal ferryboat and relaxed for a few minutes before the up-hill hike to fan out and assume security positions. We stared in envy as supply truck drivers began the climb up the fifteen-hundred-foot outpost.

Cowboy, Rabbi, Doc, and I found our small bunker on the second ring of defense about eight hundred feet above the river. We unloaded gear. Cowboy began to scratch. "Jesus. I got bugs or sumpin, Doc."

"Take off your flack jacket and shirt. I'll have a look."

Sunlight still splashed across the top half of the hill so the three of us gathered around to have a look. At first, it looked like Cowboy wore two T-shirts. He took off the first one but his upper body was still green. Warm sweat had washed the cheap dye out of cheap cotton and into his skin.

"Pull your pants and shorts down Cowboy."

He did.

Rabbi laughed. "Holy Shit. It's the Incredible Hulk! Except for your dick, Cowboy."

"Fuck you. Take your shirt off."

He did.

We did.

Four green grunts.

Doc pointed at my radio. "Mac, call the CP. Then get the infirmary on Battalion Net. If Cowboy is allergic, others will be."

Cowboy smiled and stopped scratching. "Guess I gotta go to China Beach for quarantine, huh Doc? I might be contagious. "

Rabbi pulled up his pants. "Probably poisoned Viet Cong dye. Your dick's gonna fall off."

"Yours is already gone, Pee Wee."

Well, between Rabbi getting shot in the ass for exposing Bulls Eye Brand Boxer Shorts and a dozen green grunts with allergic reaction on their private parts, most of us stopped wearing under wear of any kind. Eventually the dye wore off... but not the paranoia.

Yes, confess: I don't wear underwear and had lunch at a sunny outdoor café in my swimsuit where my balls must have slipped out. Some frustrated housewife called the cops, and now I'm on the way to jail in this police cruiser for indecent exposure.

No, the VC didn't get me. But they're still out there... waiting.

III

Seasoning

Marin County, CA

Ongoing…

He pushed the half-empty bottle of Colonel Taylor across the table.

"Join me?"

Outside in the backyard the party raged on. As usual, I had drifted away seeking sanctuary, this time into a small kitchen.

He nodded at an open dishwasher where a column of glasses stood at attention, bottoms up. I grabbed one and sat down across from him. Older by a dozen years, he stared at me from someplace far off and in that moment, I knew him.

"Thanks." I poured a bit of whiskey into a tumbler and leaned back. The well-used chair under me protested and squeaked a note in synch with the boom box outside.

"Can't take it either?" He slid his empty glass my way and I grabbed the jug by the neck. The Colonel bowed in a salute. Mission accomplished.

I took a sip and said it. "Army?"

"Korea." He saw who I was…. "You?"

I nodded. "Marines. Vietnam."

Our shared past, different but the same, rose up and held us both. We sat there looking across a suburban kitchen table into a mirror.

He raised his shot glass in a toast. "Better dead than Red."

We laughed, and the old familiar darkness retreated.

"Some chow over there on the counter. Like Vietnamese food?"

"No. That smell of fermented fish sauce really gets to me."

"Why?"

I turned around and scouted the back door and deck outside. No civilians. The nightly fog began to creep over the ridge and down into Mill Valley from Stinson Beach.

"Well, villagers and the Cong used that sauce on everything they ate out there in the boonies, probably to kill bugs. Fermentation for three days brewed up quite a stink. They called it, "Nuoc Mam"; means fish water."

"Sounds like Korean Kim Chee."

"It wasn't hot like that. It just reeked. Anyways, nights in the jungle were so dark we couldn't see shit, might as well as had our eyes closed. We'd be laying out on ambush, all in a row and side by side. Our senses became alive, mostly hearing and smelling. I guess blind people must feel that way every day."

He placed his glass down on the table without a sound. "Go on."

"The forest got so hot and humid at night we began to sort out different scents and sounds, kinda like dogs. You know what I'm talking about."

"Yes...."

156

"Pitch black, no sounds, no forward recon post to warn us… just laying there in some kinda blind man's Hell, waiting. Everybody got nervous out there at night; us, them, monkeys, everybody. So plus the heat we sweat that nervous sweat. There's a difference, a stronger smell.

"Then it would happen, just a whiff at first… nuoc mam. That damn sauce. They were crawlin up on our position, just as scared as us and sweatin out that fermented shit. Soon as it got stronger we would fire our weapons in the direction of the smell and then duck."

He sniffed a few times and raised his arms. "Don't shoot, Brother! There's some Pizza over there on top of the stove."

Our laughter attracted a couple smoking a joint in the bushes, and the girl poked her head across the threshold into our space. "What's going on in here?"

My new friend stared at me and shook his head. Silence sent her back outside, searching for some other distraction.

He looked down into the empty shot glass. "Back in Korea we had something like that goin' on. Part of the year, ground fog was so thick you could see maybe ten foot in front of you, even during the day. We were trying to hold onto some shit ground and spent a lot of time in trenches and foxholes. I haven't thought of this for a long time. Give me the last of that rye."

The amber liquid swirled around for a moment, then became still, clear.

"In the spring, fog was actually warm, a nice blanket smothering hills all around us, perfect cover for an attack… Wait. That's all we did. Wait. We knew they were coming. It was just a question of when."

He reached across to his other hand and rubbed the stump of a missing finger. "Just like you guys, all we could do was lie there and hope for some kinda warning. And like you, we smelled something that gave them away. When we got a whiff, we opened up too."

"Kim Chee?"

"No. Something much stronger. You see, when the Chinese came down across the border they brought their herbs and shit in a medicine pouch. Every gook had one tied on his belt. Everyday they ate garlic as a cure-all. Garlic. Man, I still hate that shit."

"Jesus. They ever figure it out?"

"No. Maybe they thought we had motion detectors or something. But after a while I guess they ran out of the stuff, cause we went back to just being blind in the fog."

We sat there in silence for a while, each lost in our own foggy memories. Then it happened. We looked across the table of empty glasses, remembering.

In the same instant, a light bulb went off, not overhead on the kitchen ceiling but in our heads. As though finding a new piece in a puzzle thought solved decades ago, we smiled. "What did they smell from us?"

It didn't take long. "Shaving lotion!"

He laughed so hard his stomach jarred the table knocking Colonel Taylor over, sending him rolling toward the edge. I stood him back up. Our grins filled the room.

"How did your guys do it in 'Nam? Our Southern boys would drink anything with alcohol; liquid shoe polish, brake fluid, mostly shaving lotion. They'd stand a loaf of rough gook bread on end and poor the stuff down through it. Hillbilly Filtration, they called it."

"In 'Nam we had guys called The Aqua Velva Squad". I don't think they filtered anything, just sucked down four ounces of that 40 proof blue shit. On patrol, we made them walk rear because we could smell them up front ahead of us."

And like tripping a booby trap we stared at each other in the blazing glory of discovery. How many of our guys had triggered an ambushed while stinking from a cocktail of Old Spice?

Colonel Taylor was dead. No replacement stood tall. It wasn't gonna get better than this and we both knew it.

"Time for me to leave, Jarhead. I'm gonna collect my lady and go back over the bridge. Thank you, Brother."

"You too. Every time I have garlic I'll think of tonight. What do you think? Should we advise our generals in Iraq about shaving lotion?"

He turned around in the doorway and looked down at the recently retired Colonel Taylor and our empty glasses.

"Fuck it. It all evens out."

IV
Listening Skills
Marin, County
Ongoing…

Someone yanked on my T shirt. "Daddy lets go back to the swings."

There it was again, that far away sound. I could almost figure it out.

"Come on, Daddy. Why are you staring?"

That was it; a rope blowing in the wind and slapping on a metal flag pole. But where? Nothing in sight for two hundred meters across the exposed grassy knoll in front of us… part of me stood somewhere else, listening for something else.

"Can't you hear it, honey?"

"What, Daddy?"

A leaf tumbled in the wind and I heard each little summersault whisper across the grass. Across the field, a tree line of bamboo planted to shield neighbors from the playground, scratched in the breeze. Where was I?

"They're coming!"

I reached for something,.. something, no longer there.

"Mommy!"

She picked up our daughter in her arms and saw my hand grasping for an invisible weapon. "Let's go home. I'll drive. You take the baby."

"I'm OK."

She tried to smile. "It takes time."

Six blocks down the street we passed an elementary school with its flag flying at half mast. The rope, too tight, snapped in the wind against its metal pole.

She was crying now. "Why did they shoot King? He was the best among us."

My daughter patted her shoulder. "It's OK, Mommy."

I though of Terry King in Echo Company and as we turned the corner, I said to the windshield, "The rope's too tight."

Somewhere, someone agreed, "I know…"

Lament for Brother D
Phuket, Thailand
2007

Dear Mac,

A couple nights ago there was some gunshots coming from the big nursery next door someone walking around and capping random shots into the night. I was up and out, down the road (walkin' trail) to see where the source was. No sleep, kept checkin' the perimeter.

Mai found me sittin' on the floor in the kitchen doorway 6 a.m. coffee in hand. She hugs me and asks me what am I doing up so early?

I told her about the shooting, said I feel like I'm back in Nam. Guess my face went strange at that point as she asked me what's wrong. Hugs me tighter, nothing but tears comes out.

I'm coping, telling myself it's a good thing. Maybe shed some pounds outta that old rucksack in my head, ya?

Bro D

Dear D,

The war within continues......we can only
hope for a cease-fire. Be well, my friend.
You are seen and loved. Keep a light on in
the window (you do have windows, right?)
A poem for you...

Mac

Inside the Wire

Not too far
from the old
free fire zone,
his suburban bunker
built by native labor
and staffed with
Asian love,
stands alone
against the night.
Now
the last man standing
patrols
his past
in yesterday's moonlight
seeking Psyche's sniper
but can't...
make contact.
And under memory's assault
his elaborate perimeter
dissolves around him
while he performs

his own autopsy
on the kitchen table
washing his wounds… in his own tears

Mac

Shadows
Sarge Remembers
2008

Mac,

I received quite a few pictures from Xxxxx of this years Fox 2/5 reunion in Washington, DC and I thought I would pass them on to you to view on line when you have time.

For me one revelation was the 2nd Platoon's Machine Gun Team Cpl. Xxxxx team was in attendance. Cpl. Xxxxx went home about two weeks before Union II and he asked me "What the hell happened?."

I told him the Skipper did the right thing and wanted to prep the area with air then artillery. You know the whole story. I told him Colonel Hilgartner refused all the Skipper's request and gave him a direct order to move the company out into the open or the "meat grinder" if you will.

I told him the story in front of Major General Xxxxx, he was the CO of Fox in Xxxx. Two of Cpl. Xxxxx's men said they listened to the transmission between the Skipper and me and both said there wasn't anything I could have done to change the outcome.

With all this said I still never feel quite right because I think I could have changed the out come if I had not obeyed the Skipper's orders.

Well my friend we have talked about this same subject for years and the outcome will never change. I'm sorry you missed being at the reunion. As I see the shape of some of our brethren I fear they will not be at the next reunion.

If there is something I can do for you, let me know.

Semper Fidelis,

Sarge

Dear Sarge,

Your wife looks great and your smile fills the room as usual. Thanks so much for thinking of me and the photos...just what I was hoping for- a bit of sit rep from the reunion. I recognize some of the guys and appreciate the tour of DC... some of the scenes bring a wave of emotion and I feel tears forming in the eyes of a young man who once had a band of brothers like no other.

As for you my friend... there is a well-known story to share with you and I have changed it a little to fit our purposes here.

...A man who has lived a life of integrity and service, sits alone in his back yard as the sun goes down and shadows begin to dance across a tree line in the distance. After reviewing the many accomplishments of his life, he smiles and attempts to stand but that familiar ache pulls him back down...... the demon of regret.

In the shadows before him, a spirit appears and offers him a reward for a life well lived. "Sergeant, you can return to that moment which haunts you even now after all these years. You will be as you were then with one difference: you will have the consciousness of this time and know the consequences of choices made then. Do you want to go back?"

A little over weight and burdened still with many responsibilities, he responds as he always has,

"Let's do it!"

Instantly he is transformed into the young man he once was and around him, stand even younger Marines under his command, locking and loading in a tree line. In front of them a dry, rocky, rice paddy stretches out; a graveyard waiting. Over the radio and in a voice he can barely recognize, his beloved Captain hesitates, then says, "No prep Tony. Move out. The CP will provide cover and reserve."

His heart breaks. For the first time as a Marine, the Sergeant refuses an order. "Captain, we all know this is wrong. I just can't do it, not till Arty and Air saturate the area across and above the paddy."

Silence. Then.......

"Yes. You are right. I'll pass it up to Battalion."

.....A week later in the Stars and Stripes, a headline reads, "Operation Union II, major disaster. Hesitation results in 1st Battalion, 5th Regiment surrounded and wiped out."

Its dark and the Sergeant is again sitting in his back yard. But some thing is missing a pain so old it had become another part of him, and a companion he felt he must carry to his grave.

Shining and barely visible, the spirit stands before him in the darkness and asks, "You understand now. We can never know the consequences of changing the events of that moment or any other in the past. But you can still change your own past. You can let it go…"

The spirit dissolves into the night and with him, the Sergeant's ancient pain.

Brother, we can never really know what might have happened on that day if we had made other choices. Many of us had that gut feeling it was all wrong, and each of us is still processing in our own way... I cried more than once and at another time- called Col. Xxxxx at his retirement home in Virginia and raged.

You are still alive, fighting the good fight, have created a model family and lived a life like few others. It is enough, more than enough. Captain Graham looks down and he is so very proud of you...as am I.

Your Brother, Mac

POEMS

Chips in the Mint

"More Ice Cream Honey?"
dark, shrapnel eyes-
chocolate chips
in the mint,
stare back
Through yesterday's
green mist

inside
the kitchen wallpaper
of shiny ribbons
and jungle bamboo...
....inside Honey,
splattered bodies
of old friends
....and enemies,
wait.

back in this land,
feasting on shallow
suburban calories.
he starves-
a hungry,
empty life
surrounded,
by a banquet
of fools.

around his neighborhood bunker,
the defensive perimeter
fades away each Sunday
behind a smoke screen
of Bar-b-que'd
burning flesh.

Honey slices only
civilized meat now
carving
yesterday's
body count
into his own,
friendly fired
ribs

He's camouflaged
inside
a flak jacket of fat
unable now to bend,
baste his kill
he sighs,
surrenders-
ready to join
memories,
carved up
there-
on The Wall

Mac

John Kerry Has A Cup of Coffee

"Refill, Darlin'
or...
are you OK?"

Armed
with standard issue smile,
waitress hovers
over his sector-
of the counter.

Her civilian tongue
tastes the testimonial
on the chalkboard,
"Today's Special!
Piece of Mind"

Swift aluminum shape
glides to his cup
delivering a hot payload.
Steam rises from the brew,
blending Sunday morning sounds.

Ancient essence
in an instant
of C-ration coffee,
consumes him...
again.

His back to the wall now,

cup in both hands,
he stares across the room,
over the black pool
and scouts through
yesterday's mist
as village families
single file to
empty vacant places.

Every thing
as it should be-
every thing
as it was-
every thing
in place,
every thing...
'Out of Order'.

Double doors explode
and open
A bus boy charges,
pointing his grey tub
and rescues dirty casualties
from the morning's operation.

Busboy white
fades to army green.
Vietnamese
Boy.

From the dark crystal

in his cup,
steam swims up
burning his eyes.
"Approaching the LZ,
Lieutenant.
Your team ready?"

Behind the counter
toast burns
and closing his eyes
he shuts out the sting
of
too faithful memory.
Of fumes
from a smoke grenade
marking the landing zone.
Of team members
on board waiting,
wiping baby faces
with green sleeves.

Overhead,
an exhaust fan
hums, turns, pulls
kitchen smoke snakelike,
sliding
through the ceiling.

One hand
on counter top,
another

on starboard railing.
He leans into the night.
Propeller blades slice
the dark in-between.

"We're here LT."
He watches his hands.
One belongs to
someone else…
somewhere else.

"You want a refill - or
not Darlin?"

Two hands push
His too full cup
across the counter,
through the mist
into Now.

He hears
Another voice
answer,
"No thanks.
I've had enough."

John McCain Pretends
Maverick

Dad's fault…
maybe Grandpa's.
But I showed 'em!
North Vietnamese beating me?
No problem.
I just relaxed,
felt the legacy
of Admiral McCain

Torture?
Familiar family territory.
Bombing Hanoi?
Women and children?
I imagined
my family estate,
below.

Shot down, floating
in that famous rice paddy?
Ah, born again,
baptized,
free of expectations.

Five years captive?
A gift of penance
to expiate
the sins of this Son
miscast

as heir apparent.

Here in my portable cell
still a prisoner,
I fight on,
always counter punching,
fighting ghosts,
warrior without a war.

The gooks?
My friends…
they could have broken me
with just a little-
kindness.

Mac

Sons of Abraham

This Gaza trip
The knives of our Fathers
Carve out
This silent space
Between men.
This separation from God:
Our original sin,
Cast us out
From Eden
And we turn our backs
On paradise.
Someone else
Now lives our lives..
Locked inside.
Mad Men pace,
Feet tick-tocking
In circles,
Protecting….
Nothing.
-On the long road back
To segregated Bethlehem,
Brother slays brother
And we watch
our self -inflicted wound
Bleed out into a gutter
Along this common artery
Reunited.
at last
Mac

Welcome Home

Only the feathers floating round the hat
Showed anything more spectacular had
occurred
Than the usual drowning…
The police preferred to ignore
The confusing aspects of the case
And the witnesses ran off to a PTA meeting

So the report filed and forgotten
in the archives, simply read, "Drowned"
but it was wrong: Icarus
Had swum away coming at last to a city
Where he rented a house and tended the
garden…

That nice Mr. Smith the neighbors call him
Never dreaming that the gray respectable
suit
Concealed arms that had controlled huge
wings
Nor that the sad, defeated eyes had once
Compelled the sun. And that had he told
them
They would have answered with a shocked,
uncomprehending stare….

No, he could not disturb their neat front
yards

Yet all his books insisted this was a horrible
mistake:
What was he doing in the suburbs?
Can the genius of the hero fall
To the middling stature of
the merely talented?...

And nightly, Mr. Smith probes his wound
And daily in his workshop, curtains
carefully drawn
Constructs small wings and tries to fly
To the lighting fixture on the ceiling:
Fails every time and
Hates himself for trying...

He had thought himself a hero, had acted
heroically
But now rides in carpools
Serves on various committees
and wishes –
he had drowned.

Adapted from, *Icarus*
Edward Fields, 1952

The Long Road Home

Broken home
Left alone
Fled the known
All those clones
Marine Corps
Peace Corps
Life Taker
Life Saver
Bullet holes
Broken hearts
Divine goddess
Total loss
Sahara nights
Jungle rites
Non-profits
NGOs
Bureaucrats
Same ole crap
Family man
American plan
Homeowner
Sudden loner
Faraway places
Same ole faces
Lone Ranger
Stoic stranger
Hitchhiker
Demon biker
Workshops, books

Spiritual crooks
Born again
Died again
Peyote eater
Soul seeker
Public service
Drunken menace
Activist, Catalyst
Union socialist
Ashrams
Communes
Esoteric schools
Gurus
Shamans
Charlatans
& Fools
Revelation
Incarnation
Transformation
Disintegration
Knew It All.....
Before the Fall
Lonely hiker
Pied Piper
Golden years
Fewer fears
Another cycle
Peace somehow
In this circle
Here and now

                    Mac

EPILOGUE

Hemmingway and John Wayne betrayed us and will continue to do so. There is no moment of truth just before death, no glory, and no graduation into manhood through baptism under fire. No, there is only trauma, and for survivors - the aftermath.

What *do* soldiers learn in combat? We learn how it feels to kill, how it feels to die, and for some, how it feels to die and return to life. The truly fortunate, truly blessed, experience the real moment of truth: how it feels to save a life.

Finding our way back home can take decades. The loyalty and fellowship we discovered with others in combat can ease our transition as we seek out comrades and support each other on this newest mission: winning back our own hearts and minds. This brotherhood and its magical bond, is perhaps the only meaningful legacy we shall ever inherit from that distant land.

Much has been said and written about the value of helping others. It saved my life. When ready, reaching out to others may be the best therapy available to our returning young men and women.

And still, for every new generation of American youth, the unasked questions; what *is* good, bad, right or wrong? Why? What is worth fighting for, killing for, and... yes, what will you die for?

"Teach your children well..."

ABOUT THE BOOK

Winning the War Within is the story of an ordinary American caught of in the stormy decade of the 1960s. We follow him as he fails to avoid the draft, volunteers for the Marines and finds Shangri La in the midst of chaos and destruction. Changed forever and unable to reenter his own community, he seeks to understand personal transformation through serving others as they navigate their own challenges of Post Traumatic Stress Disorder.

ABOUT THE AUTHOR

A decorated and wounded Marine in Vietnam, Brent MacKinnon returned to work in a dozen third world countries and in the US with refugees, immigrants and Native Americans. He taught language, culture and developed social service programs from elementary school to university level and served twice tours in the Peace Corps. Brent now lives in Hawaii where he is in recovery from the New Age Movement in California.

CPSIA information can be obtained at www.ICGtesting.com
Printed in the USA
LVOW07s2232121015

457926LV00033B/1527/P